The Best of

COOKING with **SHOTGUN RED**

VOLUME 1

Is this the *BEST* Cookbook?
If it ain't...
It ought to be!

Jennifer Bruce and Miss Sheila Keeton

SGR
PUBLISHING

Paperback ISBN: 978-1-7360484-0-5
eBook ISBN: 978-1-7360484-1-2
Hardback ISBN: 978-1-7360484-2-9

Editor: Donna Wilms
Recipe photography by Jennifer Bruce and Miss Sheila Keeton
Cover and design by Jennifer Bruce

www.Shotgunred.com

CONTENTS

Preface

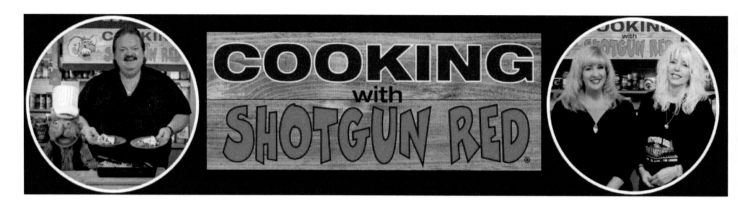

The popular YouTube Channel, "Cooking with Shotgun Red", was created by television personality, entertainer, musician, comedian, and creator of the world-famous Shotgun Red character, Steve Hall. He loved to make people laugh, entertain, and he loved to cook. He started filming the cooking show in 2014 aboard the Miss Sheila Houseboat in Nashville, Tennessee.

Steve opened every show with his famous quote, "Hunter, fisher, trapper, trader, guide, scout, interpreter, and just a country cook, Steve Hall", and closed every show with, "Is this the best? If it ain't... it ought to be!". Before Steve Hall passed away in December 2018, he had uploaded 307 recipes to the Cooking with Shotgun Red channel. Since his passing, people around the world are still discovering all of these great recipes as Cooking with Shotgun Red continues to grow each year.

Steve's wish was to make sure his cooking show kept going. After his passing, Steve's co-host, and fiancé, Miss Sheila, decided to carry on his legacy. Sheila asked their longtime friend, and Shotgun Red band member, Jennifer Bruce to help and be her new co-host. Jennifer worked with Steve in the Shotgun Red show for over 14 years. She was a featured vocalist in his stage show, managed the "Shotgun Red Variety Show" for RFDTV, and was a longtime friend to both of them. Miss Sheila and Jennifer are creating new shows, sharing new recipes, entertaining folks, and continuing to share Steve's love of cooking. Steve started this cookbook, but never had an opportunity to complete it. Miss Sheila and Jennifer decided to finish Steve's cookbook and share some of the best Cooking with Shotgun Red recipes! He would be so proud!

You can find out more by visiting **www.Shotgunred.com**

Acknowledgments

Thank you **Donna Wilms, "Momma Donna"** for your dedication, all of your hard work in helping with recipes, cooking, and editing. We couldn't have done this without you.

Thank you to **Marge Holland, "Mama Marge"** for sharing your wonderfully delicious recipes on the show over the years, and letting us share them in this cookbook. There's nothing like Mom's cooking!

Last but not least, thank you to all of our **YouTube Subscribers** and **Social Media Followers** for all of your encouragement, and continuing to support us on Cooking with Shotgun Red.
Jennifer and Miss Sheila

This book is Dedicated to The Legendary

Steve Hall "Shotgun Red"

Dec. 1, 1954 to Dec. 29, 2018

Shotgun Red is a puppet created by Steve Hall, a native of Brainerd, Minnesota. He was best known as co-host for the television talk show "Nashville Now", often appearing and adding comedy bits alongside the show's host, Ralph Emery.

The puppet, was discovered by Steve in a Minnesota hobby shop in 1980. He first used Shotgun Red as the emcee for his band at the time, Southbound '76. After traveling to Nashville to compete in the final round of The Seagrams 7 Battle of the Bands Contest, Steve and Shotgun Red crashed Ralph Emery's local morning TV show. Ralph fell in love with the little puppet, and later made him his co-host on TNN's popular talk show, "Nashville Now", which aired from 1983-1993.

Steve Hall along with his little buddy Shotgun Red, went on to appear on the television variety show, "Hee Haw" regularly for ten years. Steve hosted The Nashville Network's very first music video show "Country Clips" for six years. During that time, Shotgun Red interviewed many country artists, including Garth Brooks, Randy Travis, and many more.

Steve Hall and his co-host Miss Sheila, created their own television show on RFD TV called the "The Shotgun Red Variety Show". It aired for 4 seasons from 2011 through 2014. The show featured a variety of known and unknown acts from around the country.

In addition to touring around the world, Steve Hall and The Shotgun Red Show were the longest featured act aboard the world-famous "General Jackson Showboat" in Nashville, Tennessee. His very popular 8-piece country comedy show performed the midday cruise for over 15 years.

Steve enjoyed hunting, fishing, and always loved to cook. He wanted to share his love of cooking, so in 2014 he created his YouTube channel, "Cooking with Shotgun Red". He filmed the first shows aboard the 80 ft. houseboat he built and named after his longtime partner, fiancé, "Miss Sheila". Steve was larger than life, one of a kind, and left an unforgettable legacy.

Kitchen Conversions

TEASPOON	TABLESPOON	CUPS	MILLILITERS	FLUID OUNCES
1 tsp	1/3 tbsp	1/48 cup	5 ml	1/8 oz
3 tsp	1 tbsp	1/16 cup	15 ml	1/2 oz
6 tsp	2 tbsp	1/8 cup	30 ml	1 oz
12 tsp	4 tbsp	1/4 cup	59 ml	2 oz
16 tsp	5 1/3 tbsp	1/3 cup	79 ml	2 2/3 oz
24 tsp	8 tbsp	1/2 cup	118 ml	4 oz
32 tsp	10 2/3 tbsp	2/3 cup	158 ml	5 1/3 oz
36 tsp	12 tbsp	3/4 cup	177 ml	6 oz
48 tsp	16 tbsp	1 cup	237 ml	8 oz

FAHRENHEIT	CELSIUS
275 F	140 C
300 F	150 C
325 F	165 C
350 F	177 C
375 F	190 C
400 F	200 C
425 F	220 C
450 F	230 C
475 F	245 C
500 F	260 C

MEAT TEMPERATURE GUIDE	
Beef	@ 140 = rare @ 160 = medium @ 170 = well done
Pork	ground @ 160 = safe roast @ 165 = safe
Whole Chicken	@ 180 = safe
Whole Turkey	@ 180 = safe
Lamb Roast	@ 145 = safe

a pinch = 1/8 teaspoon

3 teaspoon = 1 tablespoon

4 tablespoons = 1 cup

2 cups = 1 pint

2 pints = 1 quart

4 quarts = 1 gallon

8 quarts = 1 peck

4 pecks = 1 bushel

SUBSTITUTION LIST

INGREDIENT	AMOUNT	SUBSTITUTION
Allspice	1 teaspoon	1/2 tsp cinnamon, 1/4 tsp ginger, and 1/4 tsp cloves
Baking powder	1 teaspoon	1/4 tsp baking soda + 1/2 tsp cream of tartar OR 1/4 tsp baking soda + 1/2 cup buttermilk (decrease liquid in recipe by 1/2 cup)
Beer	1 cup	1 cup nonalcoholic beer OR 1 cup chicken broth
Bread crumbs	1 cup	1 cup cracker crumbs OR 1 cup matzo meal OR 1 cup ground oats
Broth (beef or chicken)	1 cup	1 bouillon cube + 1 cup boiling water OR 1 tbls soy sauce + enough water to make1 cup OR 1 cup vegetable broth
Brown sugar	1 cup packed	1 cup white sugar + 1/4 cup molasses & decrease the liquid in recipe by 1/4 cup OR 1 cup white sugar
Butter	1 cup	1 cup shortening OR 7/8 cup vegetable oil OR 7/8 cup lard
Chervil	1 tbsp chopped fresh	1 tbsp chopped fresh parsley
Chicken base	1 tablespoon	1 cup canned or homemade chicken broth or stock. Reduce liquid in recipe by 1 cup
Corn syrup	1 cup	1 1/4 cup white sugar plus 1/3 cup water OR 1 cup honey OR 1 cup light treacle syrup
Cottage cheese	1 cup	1 cup farmer's cheese OR 1 cup ricotta cheese
Cream (half and half)	1 cup	7/8 cup milk plus 1 tbsp butter
Cream (heavy)	1 cup	1 cup evaporated milk OR 3/4 cup milk + 1/3 cup butter
Cream (light)	1 cup	1 cup evaporated milk OR 3/4 cup milk plus 3 tbsp butter
Cream (whipped)	1 cup	1 cup frozen whipped topping, thawed
Cream cheese	1 cup	1 cup pureed cottage cheese OR 1 cup plain yogurt, strained overnight in a cheesecloth
Cream of tartar	1 teaspoon	2 tsp lemon juice or vinegar
Egg	1 whole	2 1/2 tbsp of powdered egg substitute + 2 1/2 tbsp water OR 1/4 cup liquid egg substitute OR 1/4 cup silken tofu pureed OR 3 tbsp mayonnaise OR half a banana mashed with 1/2 tsp baking powder OR 1 tbsp powdered flax seed soaked in 3 tbsp water
Evaporated milk	1 cup	1 cup light cream
Fats for baking	1 cup	1 cup applesauce OR 1 cup fruit puree
Flour (Bread Flour)	1 cup	1 cup all-purpose flour + 1 tsp wheat gluten
Flour (Cake Flour)	1 cup	1 cup all-purpose flour minus 2 tbsp
Flour (Self-Rising)	1 cup	7/8 cup all-purpose flour + 1 1/2 tsp baking powder & 1/2 tsp of salt
Garlic	1 clove	1/8 tsp garlic powder OR 1/2 tsp granulated garlic OR 1/2 tsp garlic salt (reduce salt in recipe)
Gelatin	1 tbsp	granulated 2 teaspoons agar agar
Green onion	1 cup chopped	1 cup chopped onion, OR 1 cup chopped leek OR 1 cup chopped shallots
Hazelnuts	1 cup whole	1 cup macadamia nuts OR 1 cup almonds
Honey	1 cup	1 1/4 cup white sugar + 1/3 cup water OR 1 cup corn syrup OR 1 cup light treacle syrup

APPETIZERS

BEER BATTERED ONION RINGS

INGREDIENTS:

- Sweet Onions
- 2 Cups All-Purpose Flour
- ¼ Cup Corn Starch
- 1 Tsp. Paprika
- 1 Tsp. Salt
- ½ Tsp. Baking Powder
- ½ Tsp White Pepper
- 1 Cup Cold Beer
- Vegetable Oil

Prep. time:
35 min

Total time:
12 min

Serves: 4

"Hit them with a light dusting of salt as soon as they come out of the oil. Let them rest for a minute or two and serve hot!"-
Steve Hall

DIRECTIONS:

1. Peel the onions, then cut off the ends and slice them about ⅜ inch thick.
2. Punch out the rings, and soak them in ice cold water with some ice cubes and 1 heaping tsp. of salt for 20 to 30 minutes. In a shallow bowl, add 1 cup all-purpose flour. Then dredge the onion rings in the flour, place them on a rack, and let set for 30 minutes so the flour will stick to the onion rings.
3. Make a batter. In a bowl add 1 cup all-purpose flour, corn starch, paprika, salt, baking powder, white pepper and mix together. Slowly add very cold beer and mix until the batter is a little thinner than pancake batter.
4. In a deep fry pan, add vegetable oil (about 1 1/2 inch deep) and heat to 350 degrees. Dip the onion rings into the batter (using a chopstick, wooden skewer or fork). Let them soak in the batter until the batter sticks to the flour already on the onion rings. Drop them in the oil, and cook until nice and golden brown. Remove and place them on a bed of paper towels and serve!

JALAPEÑO SWEET CORN DIP

INGREDIENTS:

- 1 12oz. Package Frozen Sweet Corn (thawed)
- 1 Cup Grated Parmesan Cheese
- 1 Cup Shredded Mexican Blend Cheese
- 1 Cup Sour Cream
- ¼ Cup Sweet and Spicy Pickled Jalapeno Peppers
- ¼ Stick Butter
- 1 ½ Cups Butter Crackers (crushed - we use Ritz)
- Nonstick Cooking Spray

It's great for gatherings. Serve with your favorite crackers!

Prep. time:
15 min

Total time:
30 min

Serves: 6-8

DIRECTIONS:

1. Preheat oven to 350 degrees.

2. In a medium bowl, add in sweet corn, Parmesan cheese, Mexican blend cheese, sour cream, and sweet and spicy pickled jalapeño peppers. Mix together in the bowl, then spoon into a 9-inch pie plate sprayed with nonstick cooking spray.

3. In a small bowl, mix together crushed butter crackers and melted butter. Spread over the top of the corn dip.

4. Bake in the oven for 25 to 30 minutes, or until the crackers start to brown around the edge.

BRUSCHETTA ON TOASTED FRENCH BREAD

INGREDIENTS:

- French Bread
- 10 Roma Tomatoes
- ½ Cup Fresh Basil (chopped)
- 1 Tsp. Oregano
- 2 Tbsp. Minced Garlic
- 1 Tbsp. Lemon Juice
- ¼ Cup Olive Oil
- 4 Tbsp. Butter
- 4 Tbsp. Olive Oil
- 1 Tbsp. Garlic Paste
- Salt and Pepper

Prep. time: 20 min | Total time: 10 min | Serves: 5-6

DIRECTIONS:

1. Dice 10 medium Roma tomatoes into ¼ inch cubes. Place them in a medium to large bowl, and add fresh chopped basil, oregano, minced garlic, lemon juice, olive oil, and a pinch of salt and pepper. Mix lightly and chill for 15 minutes.

2. Slice the French bread at an angle. Brush both sides of the bread with a mixture of melted butter, olive oil, and garlic paste. Then brown on a griddle, or in a pan, and let them cool on a bed of paper towels.

3. Top each slice with a spoonful of the tomato mixture just before serving.

WORLD'S BEST SMOKED SALMON DIP

INGREDIENTS:

- 4 Cups Chopped Smoked Skinless Salmon (or Canned Salmon)
- 2 8oz. Packages Cream Cheese (softened)
- ½ Cup Sour Cream
- 1 Tbsp. Pepper
- 1 Tbsp. Chives
- 2 Tsp. Dill
- ¼ Cup Red Onion (diced)
- ½ Tsp. Lemon Zest
- 1 Tbsp. Lemon Juice
- 2 Tsp. Garlic Powder
- 2 Drops Worcestershire Sauce
- 1 Tbsp. Wasabi

Prep. time: 10 min | Chill time: 2 hrs | Serves: 8

DIRECTIONS:

1. In a bowl, add all ingredients except for the Salmon. Blend everything together so it's mixed well.
2. Then fold in 4 cups chopped smoked skinless salmon and mix together.
3. Chill in the refrigerator for a couple of hours, and it's ready to serve with your favorite crackers.

ANGELED EGGS (NOT THEM DEVILED ONES)

Prep. time: 10 min

Total time: 10 min

Serves: 8

INGREDIENTS:

- 1 Dozen Eggs
- 3 Tbsp. Mayonnaise
- 3 Tbsp. Sour Cream
- 1 Tbsp. Dijon Mustard
- 1 to 2 Tbsp. Sweet Pickle Relish
- 1/8 Tsp. Ground Red Pepper
- 1 Tsp. Paprika
- 1 Tsp. Soft Butter
- 1 Tbsp. Finely Chopped Sweet Onion
- 3 Tbsp. Cooked Crumbled Bacon

DIRECTIONS:

1. Put 1 dozen eggs in cold water on the stove on high. When it comes to a boil start timing... 8 minutes later remove the eggs from the boiling water and put them in a bowl of ice water. After 1 minute peel them.
2. Take the 1 dozen hard boiled eggs and cut them in half lengthwise. Put all the egg yolks in a bowl and mash well with a fork. Then add mayonnaise, sour cream, Dijon mustard, sweet pickle relish, ground red pepper, paprika, soft butter, finely chopped sweet onion, crumbled bacon, and mix well.
3. Put the mixture in a plastic zip bag and cut one of the corners of the bag, then squeeze the mixture into the egg whites.
4. Garnish with a sprinkle of paprika, and crumbled bacon.
5. Chill in the refrigerator for at least 1 hour then serve!

DEEP FRIED RAVIOLI

Prep. time:
15 min

Total time:
12 min

Serves: 4

INGREDIENTS:

- 2 9oz. Packages Cheese Ravioli
- 1 Cup Buttermilk
- 1 Cup Italian Seasoned Breadcrumbs
- Vegetable Oil
- Finely Shredded Parmesan Cheese
- Marinara Sauce

"If you really want the breadcrumbs to stick, just put them in the refrigerator for about 15 minutes.
You will love this easy appetizer for any party."-Steve Hall

DIRECTIONS:

1. Cook the Ravioli according to the directions on the package. Then drain them and let the Ravioli cool to room temperature. They are soft at this point so handle gently.
2. Place them in a bowl and pour 1 cup of buttermilk over them. Let the excess drip off, then gently dredge them in Italian seasoned breadcrumbs. Once they are coated, let them set for 5 to 10 minutes to help the breadcrumbs stick better.
3. In a deep fry pan, add about 1 - 2 inches vegetable oil. Heat the oil to 325 - 350 degrees. Deep fry small batches of the Ravioli until golden brown. Then place them on a plate lined with paper towels to cool.
4. While they are still hot, sprinkle finely shredded Parmesan cheese on top. Serve with Marinara sauce.

BREAKFAST

BEST HOMEMADE PANCAKES EVER

INGREDIENTS:

- 1 ½ Cups All-Purpose Flour
- 2 Tbsp. Sugar
- 2 Tsp. Baking Powder
- ½ Tsp. Baking Soda
- ½ Tsp. Salt
- 2 Eggs
- 2 Tbsp. Canola Oil (for pancake batter)
- 1 Stick Butter
- 1 Tsp. Pure Vanilla Extract
- 1 ½ Cups Whole Milk
- Canola Oil (use to lightly grease the griddle)
- Serve with softened Butter, Pure Maple Syrup and Powdered Sugar

"This is Sheila's Grandmother's recipe. She always said to make sure that you use real butter!"
-Steve Hall

Prep. time:
10 min

Total time:
10 min

Serves: 4

DIRECTIONS:

1. In a large bowl, whisk together the flour, sugar, baking powder, baking soda, and salt. Then add the eggs, canola oil, 2 tbsp. slightly cooled melted butter, pure vanilla extract, and whole milk. Blend all ingredients with an electric hand mixer for about 1 minute (batter will be smooth and not too thick...a few lumps are okay...so don't over mix it).

2. Pour a little canola oil on the griddle and preheat the griddle on medium heat. Pour a small amount of the batter on the hot griddle and use a spoon to spread batter into pancake size rounds. Cook pancakes until there are bubbles around the edges and a few bubbles in the middle. Check to see if golden brown, then flip them over with a spatula. Place a pat of butter on top of each pancake to melt while the underside cooks until golden brown.

3. Serve with powdered sugar and pure maple syrup, or your favorite toppings.

CHOCOLATE GRAVY AND BISCUITS

INGREDIENTS:

- 1 Cup Self-Rising Flour
- 2 Cups Sugar
- 2 Tbsp. Unsweetened Cocoa Powder
- 1 Cup Whole Milk
- 3 Cups Water
- Canned Biscuits
- Butter

Prep. time:
10 min

Total time:
10 min

Serves: 4

DIRECTIONS:

1. In a large saucepan, whisk together flour, sugar and cocoa powder. Then pour in the milk and water and stir until blended.
2. Turn the stove burner on to medium heat and stir the gravy until it is a creamy consistency.
3. Remove from heat and let sit for a minute or two and it will continue to thicken.
4. Then pour over hot buttered biscuits (baked according to package directions).

"Miss Sheila was raised on this. If you don't have homemade biscuits, you can use canned (whomp) biscuits. This southern classic is delicious...kids from one to ninety-two will love it!"-Steve Hall

---

BREAKFAST SKILLET TOPPED WITH BISCUITS

INGREDIENTS:

- 4 Tbsp. Butter
- 1 Tsp. Vegetable Oil
- ¼ Cup Sweet Yellow Onion (diced)
- ¼ Cup Red Bell Pepper (diced)
- ⅓ Cup Sliced Mushrooms
- ½ Cup Potato Hash Brown Patties (chopped up)
- ¼ Cup Smoked Sausage or Hot Dog (diced)
- 12 Eggs
- 1 Can of Biscuits
- 1 Cup Shredded Cheddar Cheese

Prep. time: 10 min

Total time: 15 min

Serves: 4

DIRECTIONS:

1. Preheat oven to 375 degrees.

2. In a cast iron skillet on medium heat, add oil and melt butter. Then add onions, red bell peppers, mushrooms, potato hash brown patties and smoked sausage or hotdog and cook until vegetables are soft.

3. Add 12 eggs (do not whisk them) into the skillet and stir them into the vegetable and sausage mixture. Cook on medium heat until edges of the eggs set slightly, then using a spatula start folding and pushing the eggs from one side of the pan to the other until the eggs are soft scrambled (they will finish cooking in the oven).

4. Sprinkle cheddar cheese over the eggs, then separate the biscuits and put them on top.

5. Bake at 375 degrees for 12 to 15 minutes, or until biscuits are golden brown. Baste the biscuits with melted butter and serve.

RHODE ISLAND JOHNNY CAKES

INGREDIENTS:

- 2 Cups Stone Ground White Corn Meal
- ½ Tsp. Salt
- 1 Tbsp. Sugar
- 1 Cup Boiling Hot Water
- Corn Oil or Bacon Grease
- 4 Tbsp. Butter
- 3 Tbsp. Pure Maple Syrup
- ½ Cup Whipped or Softened Butter
- Powdered Sugar

Prep. time:
10 min

Total time:
10 min

Serves: 4

DIRECTIONS:

1. In a bowl, add cornmeal, salt and sugar and whisk together. Then slowly pour in 1 cup of boiling hot water (maybe a bit more) and mix together until the batter is like smooth, creamy mashed potatoes.

2. Pour a little corn oil or bacon grease on a griddle and preheat on medium to medium-high. Spoon batter onto the hot griddle and spread into a round shape with the spoon. While the Johnny Cakes are cooking, add a couple spoons of butter on the griddle and let the butter melt around the outside edges.

3. Using a spatula, flip the Johnny Cakes over when the outside edges are crispy golden brown, then continue cooking until the other side is also golden brown. Place them on a serving plate, and set aside.

4. In a small bowl, stir together the whipped or softened butter and pure maple syrup. Spread on each Johnny Cake and sprinkle with powdered sugar.

EVERYTHING BREAKFAST BURRITO CASSEROLE

INGREDIENTS:

- 3 Tbsp. Butter
- 2 Tbsp. Olive Oil
- ½ Tsp. Salt
- ½ Tsp. Pepper
- Nonstick Cooking Spray
- 4 Large Flour Tortillas
- 1 Bag Frozen Potatoes O'Brien
- 1 Dozen Eggs (scrambled)
- ½ lb. Chopped Bacon (pre-cooked or make your own)
- ½ lb. Chopped Breakfast Sausage (pre-cooked or make your own)
- 1 Medium Chopped Yellow Onion
- 1 ½ Cups Shredded Cheddar Cheese
- 1 Can Diced Tomatoes with Mild Green Chilies
- 1 Jar Medium Salsa Con Queso Cheese Sauce
- ½ Cup Chopped Green Onion
- Top with Sour Cream and Salsa

"If you are expecting a large gathering for breakfast, this is an easy delicious dish to prepare ahead of time to feed the whole bunch!" - Jennifer and Miss Sheila

Prep. time:
10 min

Total time:
30 min

Serves:
6

DIRECTIONS:

1. Preheat oven to 375 degrees.

2. Place Potatoes O'Brien on a non-stick baking sheet and spread evenly. Drizzle them with a little olive oil, season with salt and pepper, and bake for 20 minutes. Remove from the oven, and set aside.

3. While the potatoes are baking in the oven, melt 2 tbsp. butter in a non-stick skillet and scramble one dozen eggs, then remove from heat, season with salt and pepper, and set aside.

4. Put yellow onions in a covered dish with 1 tbsp. butter and cook for a couple of minutes in the microwave to soften, and set aside.

5. Spray a 9 x 13 baking dish with nonstick cooking spray.

6. Put a layer of tortillas in the bottom of the baking dish. Then start layering and add in potatoes, scrambled eggs, pre-cooked bacon, pre-cooked sausage, yellow onions, shredded cheddar cheese, and diced tomatoes with mild green chilies.

7. Top it with a layer of tortillas. Then pour cheese sauce on top and spread it evenly. Sprinkle with chopped green onions.

8. Bake in the oven for 30 minutes. Cut into squares, and serve with sour cream and salsa!

SAUSAGE GRAVY AND BISCUITS

INGREDIENTS:

- 1 lb. Breakfast Sausage
- 4 Tbsp. Butter
- 4 Tbsp. Flour
- 2 Cups Whole Milk
- 1 Can of Biscuits
- Salt and Pepper

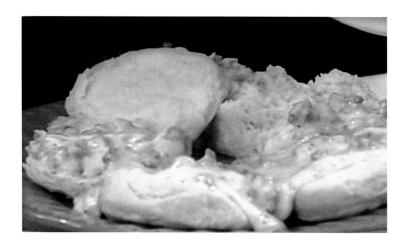

"This is a great recipe for hunting camp or camping!"- Steve Hall

---

Prep. time:
15 min

Total time:
15 min

Serves: 4

DIRECTIONS:

1. Bake the can of biscuits according to package directions.
2. In a skillet on medium heat, brown the breakfast sausage, then place it into another dish, leaving some of the sausage grease in the skillet.
3. In the same skillet, melt butter and whisk in the flour. Continue whisking and cooking the flour for about 2 to 3 minutes to make a blonde roux.
4. Pour milk a little at a time into the skillet, whisking continuously until you have mixed in about 1 to 2 cups, depending on how thick you want the gravy.
5. Let gravy simmer while you continue to whisk it for about 5 minutes, then add cooked sausage back in the skillet, stir and let simmer for a few more minutes. Serve over hot biscuits. Season with salt and pepper to taste.

HOMEMADE BUTTERMILK BISCUITS

INGREDIENTS:

- 2 Cups Self-Rising Flour
- 1 Cup Buttermilk (cold)
- 1 Stick Salted Butter (cold)

Prep. time:
15 min

Total time:
15 min

Serves: 4-5

DIRECTIONS:

1. Preheat oven to 450 degrees.
2. In a bowl, add two cups of flour and whisk for about 1 minute (or you can sift the flour).
3. Add in 6 tbsp. of cold butter cut into small chunks, and blend with a pastry cutter (blender), or blending fork, until the butter pieces are about the size of a pea (you can also do this by hand).
4. Then create a small well in the middle of the flour mixture and pour in the cold buttermilk a little at a time while mixing. You do not want to overmix, just enough so that the ingredients are combined. You may need to add a little more flour if it's too sticky.
5. On a flat surface, spread a little flour and place the dough on it. Knead the dough by folding it over about 5 to 6 times until it's soft and no longer sticky. Form the dough into a ball, pat down and spread it out until it is about ½ inch to ¾ inch thick.
6. Dip a biscuit cutter into a bowl of flour, then cut out the biscuits. Place the biscuits on some parchment paper.
7. Then place all of them into a warm buttered cast iron skillet. Bake in the preheated oven for 15 minutes, or until they turn golden brown.
8. Remove from the oven and baste with butter while hot then serve!

BURGERS, SLIDERS & SANDWICHES

ULTIMATE DOUBLE CHEESEBURGER WITH SPECIAL SAUCE

INGREDIENTS:

- 2 lbs. Ground Beef (80/20)
- 8 Slices American Cheese
- 1 Large Sweet Onion (Chopped)
- 6 Tbsp. Vegetable Oil
- 2 Tbsp. Butter
- 8 Tbsp. Yellow Mustard
- 4 Leaves Iceberg Lettuce
- 1 Large Tomato (sliced)
- 1 Jar Sliced Dill Pickles
- 4 Hamburger Buns
- Salt and Pepper

Special Sauce Ingredients:
- ½ Cup Mayonnaise
- 3 Tbsp. Ketchup
- 2 ½ Tbsp. Sweet Pickle Relish
- 2 ½ Tsp. White Vinegar
- 1 Tsp. Sugar

Prep. time:

_____

Total time:

_____

Serves: 4

DIRECTIONS:

1. Mix the special sauce ingredients together in a small bowl, and set aside.

2. In a large cast iron skillet on medium heat, add 2 tbsp. of vegetable oil and 2 tbsp. of butter. When butter has melted, add chopped onions and season with a little salt and pepper. Cook until the onions are tender and golden brown. Then transfer the onions to a bowl, and set aside.

3. Split open each hamburger bun and baste the inside of both halves with vegetable oil. Place each half face down in the same cast iron skillet on medium heat and toast until light golden brown. Then remove buns from the skillet and place them on a plate.

4. On parchment paper, press and shape the ground beef into 8 patties about ¼ inch thick. In the same cast iron skillet on medium heat, add a little vegetable oil and cook one side of the patties until browned. Before you flip the patties over, season with salt and pepper and spread a thin layer of yellow mustard on each of them. Then flip the patties over and cook until browned. Season each patty with salt and pepper, then add a slice of cheese and a spoonful of grilled onions. Turn off the heat, then cover to melt the cheese.

5. Put the buns on a serving platter and spread both sides with some special sauce. On each bottom bun, place some dill pickles, then lettuce, and tomato slices. Then top with 2 of the patties, and then the top of the hamburger bun. Get ready to bite into the most mouthwatering, juiciest hamburger ever!

GRILLED BOLOGNA SLIDERS WITH CHOW CHOW RELISH

INGREDIENTS:

- 8 Slices Frozen Texas Toast with Garlic Butter
- 8 Slices Thick Bologna
- 8 Slices Cheese (your choice)
- 2 Tbsp. Spicy Brown Mustard
- 3 Tbsp. Mayonnaise
- Leafy Lettuce
- 1 Tomato (sliced thin)
- 1 Jar Mild Chow Chow Relish

Prep. time:
10 min

Total time:
10 min

Serves: 4

DIRECTIONS:

1. Put 8 slices of frozen Texas Toast on a hot griddle and cook both sides until golden brown. Then set them aside on a serving plate.
2. Take the 8 slices of "thick sliced" bologna and remove the casing on the outside edge, then make 4 small ½ inch cuts around the outside edge of each of them (spaced apart evenly for a total of 4 slices around the edges) and make a tiny cut in the center of each slice. This will help to keep the bologna slices from curling up when you are cooking them.
3. In a griddle on medium-high heat, place the slices of bologna in a single layer and cook them until golden brown on both sides (about 2 minutes per side). Turn off the griddle and add a slice of cheese on top of each slice of bologna.
4. In a small bowl, mix together the mayonnaise and spicy brown mustard.
5. Spread the mayonnaise and mustard mixture evenly on 4 of the 8 slices of Texas toast, then add some leaf lettuce, then 2 slices of cheese topped bologna, then a thin slice of tomato with some chow chow relish spread on top. Now top each slider with the other slice of Texas Toast. So Delicious!

"You can use any Chow Chow Relish if you can't find Tennessee Chow Chow Relish, but....it ain't as good!"
Steve Hall

BACON GRILLED CHEESE WITH YUM YUM SAUCE

INGREDIENTS:

Yum Yum Sauce:
- ½ Cup Mayonnaise
- ½ Tsp. Garlic Powder
- 1 Tbsp. Ketchup
- ½ Tsp. Mustard
- ½ Tbsp. Melted Butter
- ½ Tsp. Sugar
- ½ Tsp. Paprika
- A little water to thin the sauce

Sandwich Ingredients:
- Bread (4 slices - your Choice)
- 1 Stick Softened Butter
- Garlic Salt
- Cheese
    - Monterey Jack Cheese (4 slices)
    - Muenster Cheese (4 slices)
    - Cheddar Cheese (4 slices)
- Tomato (sliced thin)
- Bacon (pre-cooked)

Prep. time: 10 min

Total time: 10 min

Serves: 2

DIRECTIONS:

1. In a bowl, mix together the yum yum sauce ingredients. Then place in the refrigerator to chill while preparing the bacon grilled cheese sandwich.

2. Spread softened butter on one side of each slice of bread and sprinkle with a little garlic salt. Then place the bread slices, butter side down, on a preheated skillet on medium heat. Put 3 slices of cheese on each slice of bread. Then top two slices of the bread with pre-cooked bacon, and tomato slices. Drizzle plenty of the delicious yum yum sauce over the tomato.

3. Cook all 4 slices of bread until golden brown and cheese is melted. Then put the 2 slices of bread with cheese, on top of the 2 slices of bread with cheese, bacon, and tomato.

4. Remove from heat and eat. Yum Yum!

MEATLOAF BURGERS! (HOT OFF THE GRIDDLE)

INGREDIENTS:

- 1 lb. Ground Beef (80/20)
- 1 lb. Ground Pork
- ½ Cup of chopped (fully cooked) Honey Ham
- 2 Eggs (beaten)
- 1 Cup Pork Flavor Stuffing Mix
- ⅛ Cup Ketchup
- ½ Tsp. Sriracha Sauce
- 1 Large Tomato (sliced thin)
- ¼ Cup Olive Oil
- 1 Tsp. Minced Garlic
- 1 Medium Sweet Yellow Onion (finely diced)
- ⅛ Cup Milk
- Potato Bread Hamburger Buns
- 4 Tbsp. Butter (softened)

Creamy Cheese Sauce
- 4 oz. Cream Cheese (softened)
- ¼ Tsp. Butter (softened)
- ¼ Tsp. each - Lemon Juice, Parsley and Dill

Sugar Onions
- 1 Medium Sweet Yellow Onion (sliced into rings)
- ½ Tsp. each - White Sugar, Brown Sugar and Balsamic Vinegar
- 2 Tsp. Bacon Grease
- 1 Cup Sliced Mushrooms

Prep. time: 15 min | Total time: 20 min | Serves: 8

DIRECTIONS:

1. In a small bowl, mix together olive oil and minced garlic and heat it up on the stove in a small saucepan. Put sliced tomatoes in a shallow pan and pour the olive oil and minced garlic over the tomatoes, then set aside and let sit and marinate.

2. In a skillet on medium heat, melt bacon grease. Then add onions, white sugar, brown sugar and balsamic vinegar, and sauté the onions until they are soft. Then add mushrooms and sauté until mushrooms and onions are caramelized.

3. In a small bowl, mix together softened cream cheese, softened butter, lemon juice, parsley and dill, then set aside.

4. In a large bowl, lightly mix together the ground beef, ground pork, and chopped ham. Then add in, eggs, pork flavor stuffing mix, diced onions, ketchup, sriracha sauce, and milk. Mix together well, then place meatloaf mixture on a sheet of wax paper and shape evenly into ¼ lb. burger patties.

5. Cook the burgers on a griddle or a skillet on medium-heat until browned on both sides and done in the middle (or until 165 degrees). Remove from heat and set aside.

6. Lightly spread softened butter on the buns and brown them face down on a griddle. Then remove from heat and place them on a serving platter.

7. On each of the bottom buns, spread some of the creamy cheese sauce mixture, add a slice of the marinated tomatoes, then a meatloaf burger. Top with sugar onions and mushrooms, then cover each one with a top bun.

WORLD'S BEST ROAST BEEF SANDWICH

INGREDIENTS:

- Eye of Round Beef Roast
- 1 Tsp. Garlic Powder
- 1 Tsp. Onion Powder
- 1 Tsp. Salt
- 1 Tsp. Pepper
- 1 Pkg. Sub-Style Buns
- 1 Sliced Onion

Au Jus Ingredients:
- 4 Cups Beef Stock
- ⅛ Cup Red Wine
- ¼ Tsp. Flour
- ¼ Tsp. Sugar
- ¼ Cup Diced Carrots
- ¼ Cup Diced Celery
- ¼ Cup Diced Yellow Onion
- Salt and Pepper to Taste

Tiger Sauce
- ½ Cup Mayonnaise
- ½ Cup Sour Cream
- 2 Tbsp. Prepared Horseradish
- ½ Tsp. Dry Mustard
- ½ Tsp. Garlic Powder
- ½ Tsp. Chives
- ½ Tsp. Lemon Juice
- ½ Tsp. Dijon Mustard
- ¼ Tsp. Worcestershire Sauce

DIRECTIONS:

Prep. time: 10 min | Total time: 60 min | Serves: 4

1. Preheat oven to 300 degrees.
2. Remove the roast from the refrigerator and let it rest at room temperature for no more than 20 to 30 minutes. Then season all sides of the roast with salt, pepper, onion powder, and garlic powder.
3. Place the roast in a roasting pan on a rack and insert a meat thermometer into it at a 45 degree angle, so the tip of the thermometer is in the center of the roast.
4. Bake it in the oven at 300 degrees until the internal temperature reaches 105-110 degrees. Then remove the roast and place it on a platter. Let it rest (meat continues to cook while it rests) until the internal temperature rises to 122-125 degrees and then starts to go down in temperature before you slice it (the roast will be rare, so if you like it more well done, put a serving of the thin sliced roast in the Au Jus and let simmer for about 1 minute). Slice the roast against the grain and very thin on a meat slicer, or by hand with a sharp knife.
5. While the roast is in the oven, prepare the Tiger Sauce. In a bowl, mix together the mayonnaise, sour cream, prepared horseradish, dry mustard, garlic powder, chives, lemon juice, Dijon mustard, and Worcestershire sauce, then set aside.
6. While the roast is resting, prepare the Au Jus. Pour drippings from the roast into a pan and whisk in 1 cup of beef stock, red wine, and flour. Then add carrots, celery and onions and simmer for 5 to 10 minute. Then add the remaining 3 cups of beef stock and let simmer until it reduces by about ⅓. Strain out the vegetables, then add sugar and season with salt and pepper to taste.
7. Serve the sliced beef on a sub-style bun topped with sliced onions, Au Jus, and Tiger Sauce.

BACON WRAPPED HOT DOGS MEXICAN STYLE

Prep. time: 10 min | Total time: 15 min | Serves: 4

INGREDIENTS:

- 1 Package Thin Sliced Bacon
- 4 Bun Length Hot Dogs
- 4 Brat Buns
- 1 Stick Butter (softened)
- 1 Cup Diced Tomatoes
- ½ Cup Diced Onions
- ¼ Cup Chopped Cilantro
- Garnish with Mayonnaise, Mustard and Hot Sauce

DIRECTIONS:

1. Wrap each hot dog with 1 slice of thin bacon, and secure with toothpicks on each end.
2. Place bacon wrapped hot dogs on a griddle and cook them on medium heat until the bacon is crisp (turning them often so they will cook evenly). Then put them on a serving plate and remove the toothpicks.
3. Spread softened butter on the inside of each brat style bun, and toast on a griddle until golden brown.
4. Put a bacon wrapped hot dog inside each brat bun, then top with diced tomatoes, diced onions, cilantro, and garnish with mayonnaise, mustard and your favorite hot sauce.

CASSEROLES

ALABAMA HASHBROWN CASSEROLE

INGREDIENTS:

- 1 Pkg. 2 lbs. Frozen Hash Browns (thawed)
- 2 Cups Butter Crackers (crushed - we use Ritz)
- 1 Can Cream of Chicken Soup
- 2 Cups Sour Cream
- 1 Cup Butter (melted)
- ½ Tsp. Salt
- ½ Tsp. Pepper
- 2 Cups Medium Cheddar Cheese(shredded)
- 1 Medium Yellow Onion (finely chopped)
- Nonstick Cooking Spray

Prep. time: 10 min

Total time: 60 min

Serves: 6-8

DIRECTIONS:

1. Preheat oven to 350 degrees.
2. In a bowl, mix together the cream of chicken soup, sour cream, onions, salt and pepper and ½ cup of melted butter (reserve the other ½ cup of melted butter for the butter cracker topping).
3. Put the thawed hashbrown potatoes in a large bowl, then pour in the cream of chicken soup mixture and shredded cheese and gently mix together. Pour into a 3 quart casserole dish sprayed with nonstick cooking spray.
4. In a separate bowl, mix together the crushed butter crackers and ½ cup of melted butter.
5. Spread the butter cracker mixture evenly on top of the hashbrowns, and cover the casserole dish with aluminum foil.
6. Bake at 350 degrees for 30 minutes, then remove the foil and bake for another 30 minutes, or until the casserole is bubbling and the butter cracker topping is golden brown.

LOUISIANA CRAWFISH CASSEROLE

INGREDIENTS:

- 1 Pkg. 12oz. Cooked Crawfish Tail Meat
- 1 Can Tomato Soup
- 1 ½ Cups Instant Rice (uncooked)
- ½ Cup Green Bell Pepper (diced)
- ½ Cup Red Bell Pepper (diced)
- 1 Cup Sweet Onion (diced)
- 1 Tsp. Minced Garlic
- 2 Tsp. Vegetable Oil
- 2 Tsp. Worcestershire Sauce
- 1 Tsp. Hot Sauce
- 1 Can 8oz. Diced Tomatoes with basil, garlic and oregano
- 1 Cup Butter Crackers (crushed - we use Ritz)
- ¼ Cup Butter (melted)
- Nonstick Cooking Spray

Prep. time: 15 min | Total time: 45 min | Serves: 4

DIRECTIONS:

1. Preheat oven to 350 degrees.

2. In a bowl, mix together the tomato soup, uncooked rice, red and green bell peppers, onions, garlic, vegetable oil, Worcestershire sauce, hot sauce, and diced tomatoes with basil, garlic, and oregano. Then gently mix in the cooked crawfish tail meat, and pour and spread it into a casserole dish that has been sprayed with nonstick cooking spray.

3. In a small bowl, mix together the butter crackers with melted butter. Then spread evenly on top of the crawfish mixture.

4. Bake in the oven at 350 degrees for 35 minutes, then turn the oven to 425 degrees and bake for another 10 minutes, or until the butter cracker topping is golden brown.

LOADED CHICKEN AND BAKED POTATO CASSEROLE

INGREDIENTS:

- 1 Bag Petite Gold Potatoes (about 15-20 small potatoes)
- 1 Rotisserie Chicken (shredded)
- 1 Stick Butter (melted)
- 1 Pkg. Bacon (cooked and chopped)
- 3 Tbsp. Bacon Grease
- 1 12oz Bag Frozen Broccoli Florets (thawed)
- ¾ Cup Green Onions (chopped)
- ½ Cup Chicken Broth
- 2 Cups Sour Cream
- 1 Cup Ranch Dressing
- 2 Cups Sharp Cheddar Cheese (shredded)
- 1 Tsp. Paprika
- ½ Tsp. Salt
- ½ Tsp. Pepper
- Nonstick Cooking Spray

Prep. time: 15 min

Total time: 40 min

Serves: 6-8

DIRECTIONS:

1. Preheat oven to 375 degrees.

2. In a large pot of boiling water, add whole potatoes and about 1 tsp salt. Cook the potatoes until they are fork tender (about 20 minutes) then drain, cool and slice in half.

3. Place bacon strips on a foil lined baking sheet and cook in the oven at 400 degrees for about 20 minutes, or until crisp. Place bacon on a plate lined with paper towels and chop them up when cooled. Reserve about 3 tbsp. of the bacon grease to drizzle on the potatoes.

4. In a large bowl, add shredded chicken, chopped bacon (reserve 2 to 3 tbsp. for top of casserole), broccoli, and green onions (reserve 2 to 3 tbsp. for top of casserole), then season with salt and pepper and mix well.

5. In a separate bowl, add chicken broth, sour cream, ranch dressing, 1 cup of the shredded cheese (reserve the other cup for top of casserole), paprika, salt, pepper and stir until well blended.

6. In a separate bowl, add chicken broth, sour cream, ranch dressing, 1 cup of the shredded

cheese (reserve the other cup for top of casserole), paprika, salt, pepper and stir until well blended.

7. Spray a 9x13 baking dish with nonstick cooking spray and fill the bottom with cooked potato halves face up, then pour the melted butter and bacon grease over the potatoes.

8. Spread the shredded chicken mixture on top of the potatoes, then spread the sour cream, ranch dressing, and shredded cheese mixture on top of the chicken mixture.

9. Sprinkle the top of the casserole with remaining shredded cheese, bacon and green onion. Place in the oven and bake at 375 degrees for about 20 minutes or until the cheese has melted. Remove from the oven and Enjoy!

HOMEMADE TAMALE PIE

INGREDIENTS:

- 2 lbs. Ground Beef (85/15)
- 1 Large Yellow Onion (Diced)
- 1 Red Bell Pepper (Diced)
- 2 Tbsp. Minced Garlic
- 1 Tsp. Salt
- 1 Tsp. Pepper
- 2 Tbsp. Chili Powder
- 1½ Tsp. Cumin
- 1 Can Sweet Corn (drained)
- 2 Cups Crushed Tomatoes
- 2 Cans Diced Tomatoes with Mild Green Chilies
- 1 Tbsp. Cornstarch
- 2 Cups Shredded Mexican Blend Cheese
- 2 Cups Golden Corn Flour (Masa Harina)
- 1½ Tsp. Baking Powder
- 1 Tsp. Salt
- 1½-2 Cups Chicken Broth
- 1 Stick Salted Butter (Melted)
- Garnish with Sour Cream and Chives

| Prep. time: | Total time: | Serves: |
| 15 min | 50 min | 6 |

DIRECTIONS:

1. Preheat oven to 350 degrees.

2. In a cast iron skillet on medium heat, start browning up the ground beef, then stir in the onions, red bell peppers, and minced garlic. Season with salt, pepper, chili powder and ground cumin. Continue cooking until the ground beef has completely browned and the onions and bell peppers are tender.

3. Stir in the sweet corn, 2 cans of diced tomatoes with green chilies, 2 cups of crushed tomatoes, and add 1 tbsp. of cornstarch. Let simmer for a couple of minutes, then remove from heat and top with 2 cups of the shredded cheese. Set aside while you make the Masa.

4. In a large bowl, combine the corn flour (Masa Harina), baking powder, and salt. Mix dry ingredients together, then stir in the melted butter. Slowly pour in the chicken broth and mix with the dry ingredients until the masa mixture has a spreadable consistency like peanut butter.

5. Spread the masa mixture evenly over the top of the ground beef mixture and shredded cheese in the cast iron skillet.

6. Bake in the oven at 350 degrees for about 30 to 40 minute, or until a toothpick inserted into the center of the masa topping comes out clean and the masa topping is golden brown.

7. Remove from the oven and let it set for about 10 minutes. Then serve warm, and garnish with sour cream and chives. Mmmmm so good!!!!

AMAZING SHEPHERD'S PIE AKA COTTAGE PIE

INGREDIENTS:

- 5 Large Potatoes
- 2 lbs. Lean Ground Beef (Lamb if making true Shepherd's Pie)
- 1 Medium Chopped Onion
- 1 Tbsp. Minced Garlic
- 4 Tsp. Salt
- 2 Tsp. Black Pepper
- 2 Tsp. Garlic Powder
- 3 Tbsp. All-Purpose Flour
- 4 Tbsp. Ketchup
- 2 Tbsp. Worcestershire Sauce
- 2 Cups Beef Broth
- 1 ½ Cups Frozen Peas and Carrots (thawed)
- 1 Stick Salted Butter
- 1 Egg Yolk
- ½ Cup Cream Cheese
- ½ Cup Sour Cream
- ¼ Cup Parmesan Cheese
- Fresh Parsley
- Paprika
- Nonstick Cooking Spray

Prep. time: 15 min | Total time: 55 min | Serves: 6-8

DIRECTIONS:

1. Preheat oven to 375 degrees.
2. Clean and peel the potatoes and cut them into quarters. Then place the potatoes into a large pot and cover them with cold water. Add 2 tsp. of salt to the water. Turn the heat on high and bring to a boil, then reduce heat to medium-low or low, and put a lid on the pot. Continue cooking the potatoes in gently boiling water for about 20 minutes or until fork tender.

3. When the potatoes are fork tender, remove pot from heat and drain the potatoes well in a colander. Then pour potatoes back into the large pot and add butter, egg yolk, cream cheese and sour cream, and mash by hand with a potato masher. When they are well mashed, whip with an electric mixer until potatoes are creamy.

4. In a skillet on medium heat, add lean ground beef and chopped onions and cook until browned. Then add in 1 tbsp. minced garlic, 2 tsp. salt, 2 tsp pepper, and 2 tsp garlic powder. Stir in 3 tbsp. of flour and cook for about 2 minutes. Then add in the ketchup, Worcestershire sauce, and beef broth. Let simmer until the sauce thickens, then remove from heat and add in the thawed peas and carrots.

5. Pour the meat mixture into a 9 x 13 baking dish that has been sprayed with nonstick cooking spray. Then spoon the creamy mashed potatoes on top and spread evenly, then sprinkle with a little salt and pepper. Bake in the oven for 35 minutes, or until the potatoes start to turn golden brown.

6. Remove from the oven and top with grated parmesan cheese, then sprinkle with some paprika, and garnish with fresh parsley. Then let it sit for about 20 minutes before serving. You are going to love this classic recipe!

TATER TOT CHEESEBURGER CASSEROLE

Prep. time:
15 min

Total time:
55 min

Serves: 6

INGREDIENTS:

- 1 ½ lbs. Ground Beef (80/20)
- 1 Large 32oz. Bag Frozen Tater Tots
- 1 Bag Frozen Sweet Corn (thawed)
- 1 Yellow Onion (chopped)
- 2 Tbsp. Olive Oil
- 2 Tbsp. All-Purpose Flour
- 2 Tbsp. Worcestershire Sauce
- 3 oz Sour Cream
- 3 oz Cream Cheese (softened)
- 1 ¾ Cups Beef Broth
- 2 Cups Shredded Cheddar Cheese
- ½ Cup Green Onion or Chives
- 2 Tbsp. Minced Garlic
- ½ Tsp. Onion Powder
- ½ Tsp Garlic Powder
- ½ Tsp. Salt
- ½ Tsp. Pepper

DIRECTIONS:

1. Preheat oven to 375 degrees.
2. In a skillet on medium-high heat, add olive oil. Then add ground beef and onions, and cook until browned.
3. Drain any excess fat, then sprinkle flour on the beef mixture evenly and cook for 1 to 2 minutes. Stir in beef broth and Worcestershire sauce. Turn heat down to medium, cover and let simmer for 10 minutes.
4. Then add softened cream cheese, sour cream, and sweet corn to the beef mixture and mix together well.
5. Pour beef mixture into a 9 x 12 casserole dish sprayed with nonstick cooking spray. Then season with salt, pepper, onion powder, and garlic powder. Then add a layer of shredded cheddar cheese, and top with a layer of the tater tots. Sprinkle with some green onions.
6. Bake in the oven for 40 to 45 minutes. Let cool for 10 to 15 minutes and it's ready to serve!

CHILI, SOUPS AND STEWS

TEX-MEX CHICKEN CORN SOUP

INGREDIENTS:

- 4 Cups Cooked Shredded Chicken (seasoned with taco seasoning)
- 2 Tbsp. Olive Oil
- 1 Sweet Yellow Onion (sliced thin)
- 1 Small Jalapeno Pepper (sliced thin - ends and seeds removed)
- 1 12oz. bag Frozen Sweet Corn (thawed)
- 1½ Tsp. Chili Powder
- 4 Cups Chicken Stock
- 1 Can Diced Tomatoes with Mild Green Chilies
- 1 8oz. Can Tomato Sauce
- 1 Can White Hominy (rinsed and drained)
- ½ Tsp. Salt
- ¼ Tsp. Pepper
- ½ Tsp. White Sugar
- 1 Cup Shredded Mexican Blend Cheese
- 1 Cup Sour Cream
- 1 Bag Tortilla Chips
- Green Onions (chopped)

Prep. time:
15 min

Total time:
20 min

Serves: 6

DIRECTIONS:

1. In a Dutch oven pot on medium-high heat, add 2 tbsp. of olive oil. When the olive oil is hot, add the sliced onions and jalapeno peppers, cook until they have a golden brown color. Then add in the corn and cook it until slightly golden brown as well. Stir in the chili powder and cook for another 1 to 2 minutes.
2. Pour in the chicken stock, and add salt and pepper. Then add white hominy, diced tomatoes with green chilies, and tomato sauce, and reduce heat to medium-low and let simmer for about 2 minutes.
3. Add the cooked shredded chicken and white sugar, and simmer for about 10 minutes uncovered.
4. Serve and top with some shredded Mexican blend cheese, tortilla chips, dollop of sour cream, and chopped green onions.

SLOW COOKER BEEF STEW

INGREDIENTS:

- 2 lbs. Cubed Beef Stew Meat
- 4 Tbsp. Canola Oil
- 4 Slices of Bacon (chopped)
- 1 Cup All-Purpose Flour
- 1 Tsp. Salt
- 1 Tsp. Pepper
- 1 Tsp. Garlic Powder
- 1 tsp. Onion Powder
- ½ Cup Red Wine
- 1 Small Yellow Onion (diced)
- 1 Tbsp. Minced Garlic
- 1 Tbsp. Worcestershire Sauce
- 2 Cups Beef Stock
- 1 Cup Sliced Mushrooms
- 1 Cup Baby Carrots
- ½ Cup Celery (diced)
- 3 Red Potatoes (cut into 1½ inch chunks)
- 1 8oz. Can Tomato Sauce

Seasoning for Entire Pot

- ¼ Tsp. Parsley
- ¼ Tsp. Sage
- ¼ Tsp. Rosemary
- ¼ Tsp. Thyme
- ½ Tsp. Salt
- ½ Tsp. Black Pepper
- 1 Package Beef Gravy Mix (if you like you stew thicker)

Prep. time:
15 min

Total time:
6-8 hours

Serves: 5

DIRECTIONS:

1. In a large deep frying pan on medium heat, add in canola oil and chopped bacon. Cook bacon until done.
2. While the bacon is cooking, in a bowl add 1 cup flour, 1 tsp. salt, 1 tsp. pepper, 1 tsp. garlic powder, and 1 tsp onion powder, and whisk together.
3. Dredge beef stew meat in the seasoned flour, then add it into the large frying pan with the bacon and sear the stew meat on all sides until golden brown.
4. Then pour in the red wine and add the diced onion, minced garlic, Worcestershire sauce, and 1 cup of beef stock.
5. Pour everything from the frying pan into the crockpot/slow cooker. Then add the mushrooms, baby carrots, celery, red potatoes, tomato sauce, and 1 cup of beef stock (or enough to cover the top of the vegetables).
6. Cook for 6 hours on high or 8 hours on low.
7. Then season the entire pot with the ingredients listed, and cook for 10 more minutes. Serve and enjoy!

WHITE CHICKEN CHILI

INGREDIENTS:

- 1 Rotisserie Chicken (2 cups shredded)
- 2½ Cups Chicken Broth
- 3 Cans Great Northern Beans (drained)
- 1 Can Diced Tomatoes with Mild Green Chilies
- 1 Small Can Mild Chopped Green Chilies
- 1 Can Sweet Corn (drained)
- 1 Cup Chopped Yellow Onion
- 1 Tbsp. Minced Garlic
- 2 Tbsp. Olive Oil
- 1 Tbsp. Butter
- 1 Tbsp. Granulated Chicken Bouillon
- 1½ Tbsp. Chili Powder
- 1 Tsp. Red Pepper Flakes
- 1 Tsp. Salt
- 1 Tsp. Pepper
- 1 Cup Sour Cream
- 1 Cup Shredded Monterey Jack Cheese

Prep. time: 15 min | Total time: 4-6 hours | Serves: 6

DIRECTIONS:

1. In a crockpot, add in shredded chicken, chicken broth, 2 cans of whole drained beans, 1 can of drained beans mashed with a fork (to thicken the chili), 1 can diced tomatoes with green chilies, 1 can green chilies, 1 can drained sweet corn, and sour cream.
2. In a skillet on medium heat, add olive oil and butter. When the butter is melted, add the onions and sauté 3 to 4 minutes, then add the garlic and sauté for 1 more minute.
3. Add the sautéed onions and garlic into the crockpot. Then add granulated chicken bouillon, red pepper flakes, chili powder, salt and pepper.
4. Cover and cook on high 3 to 4 hours or on low 5 to 6 hours (add shredded cheese the last 15 minutes of cooking time).
5. Serve and top with more shredded cheese, sour cream, crispy onions, tortilla chips and garnish with cilantro.

TEXAS CHILI aka BOWL OF RED

Prep. time: 15 min | Total time: 75 min | Serves: 4

INGREDIENTS:

- 2 lbs. Ground Beef (85/15)
- 7 Strips of Bacon (chopped)
- ½ Cup Diced Yellow Onion
- ½ Cup Diced Bell Peppers (Green and Red)
- ½ Cup Diced Celery
- 2 Cans Diced Tomatoes
- 6 Roma Tomatoes (chopped)
- 1 Jalapeno Pepper (diced - remove each end and the seeds)
- ½ Cup Beef Broth
- 1 Tbsp. Minced Garlic
- ½ Tbsp. Brown Sugar
- 2 Tbsp. Chili Powder
- 1 Tbsp. Paprika
- ½ Tsp. Cumin
- 1 Tsp. Red Pepper Flakes
- ¼ Cup of Strong Brewed Coffee
- 1 Tsp. Salt
- Corn Tortillas
- Corn Chips

Garnish:
- Shredded Cheddar and Pepper Jack Cheese, Sour Cream, and Green Onions, or Chives

DIRECTIONS:

1. In a Dutch oven pot on medium heat, cook the ground beef until browned. Then drain and transfer the ground beef to a bowl, and set aside.

2. Add chopped bacon in the Dutch oven and cook on medium-low heat until browned. Leave the bacon and the bacon grease in the pot and add diced onions, diced bell peppers, and diced celery. Simmer on medium heat for 5 minutes to soften the vegetables.

3. Pour 1 can of diced tomatoes in a blender, and blend until smooth. Then add the tomatoes in the blender, 1 can of diced tomatoes (drained), ½ of the chopped Roma tomatoes, and diced jalapeño pepper into the Dutch oven pot with the bacon and the vegetables.

4. Add the browned beef back into the Dutch oven pot. Then add beef broth, garlic, brown sugar, chili powder, cumin, paprika, red pepper flakes, and strong brewed coffee. Cover and simmer for 45 to 55 minutes.

5. Season with salt, and add the rest of the diced Roma tomatoes. Simmer for another minute or two, and it's ready to serve.

6. Put a corn tortilla in the bottom of a bowl, add some chili with corn chips around the edge. Then top it with shredded cheese, a dollop of sour cream, and a sprinkle of chives.

WISCONSIN 4 CHEESE BEER SOUP

Prep. time:
15 min

Total time:
40 min

Serves: 6

INGREDIENTS:

- 6 Strips Thin Sliced Bacon
- 4 Cups Half and Half
- 4 Cups Chicken Broth
- 1 Bottle of Dark Beer
- ½ Stick Butter
- ¼ Cup Bacon Grease
- ½ Cup All-Purpose Flour
- 8 oz. Mild Cheddar Cheese (finely shredded)
- ¼ Cup Parmesan Cheese (grated)
- 6 oz. Provolone Cheese (sliced)
- 6 oz. Pepper Jack Cheese (sliced)
- 1 Tsp. Dry Mustard
- 1 Tsp. Chicken Broth Base & Seasoning

- 1 Tsp. Paprika
- 1 Tsp. Garlic Powder
- 1 Tsp. Onion Powder
- 1 Tsp. Salt
- 1 Tsp. Pepper
- Hot Sauce (2 to 3 drops)

Garnish:
- Shredded Cheddar Cheese
- Crispy Bacon Bits
- Chives.

As Shotgun Red would say, "It's Fan..Tabulous!" - Steve Hall

DIRECTIONS:

1. Place bacon in a cold frying pan without overlapping. Cook on medium-low heat and turn bacon with tongs occasionally so it cooks evenly. Cook until bacon is crispy, then transfer bacon to a plate lined with paper towels. When bacon has cooled off, chop into small bits and set aside for the soup topping. Reserve ¼ cup of bacon grease for the roux.

2. In a large stock pot or Dutch oven on medium heat, add butter and bacon grease. When the butter is melted, add in flour and whisk continuously for 8 to 10 minutes, or until the flour is cooked and the roux is creamy and a blond color.

3. Slowly stir in slightly warmed half and half, and chicken broth, and add dry mustard and paprika. Then add cheddar cheese, pepper jack cheese, provolone cheese, and parmesan cheese. Pour in a bottle of beer and bring to a simmer on medium-low heat and continue to stir until all the cheese has melted and the soup is creamy.

4. Add chicken broth base seasoning, garlic powder, onion powder, salt, pepper, and a couple of drops of hot sauce. Simmer for a few more minutes and it's ready to enjoy.

5. Serve with chunks of bread or in a bread bowl and top with a sprinkle of shredded cheddar cheese, chives, and crispy bacon bits.

LOADED POTATO SOUP

Prep. time: 15 min | Total time: 45 min | Serves: 5

INGREDIENTS:

- 4 Potatoes (peeled and cut into small cubes)
- 1½ Cups Cheddar Cheese
- ½ Cup Sour Cream
- 3 Cups Whole Milk
- 3 Cups Chicken Stock
- 8 Slices of Bacon (chopped)
- 4 Tbsp. Butter
- 4 Tbsp. All-Purpose Flour
- 1 Yellow Onion (finely diced)
- ½ Tsp. Salt
- ½ Tsp. Peppers
- Garnish with Chopped Green Onions

DIRECTIONS:

1. In a large pot, cook the bacon on medium heat until crispy, then place the bacon on a plate with paper towels and set aside.
2. Then add butter in the pot with the bacon grease. When the butter is melted, add onions and sauté for 2 to 3 minutes until tender.
3. Add flour and stir constantly with a whisk for 2 minutes until flour is cooked.
4. Pour in the milk (stirring constantly) and then the chicken stock, and bring to a simmer
5. Then add the potatoes, partially cover with a lid and simmer for another 20 minutes, or until potatoes are fork tender.
6. Add in sour cream, cheddar cheese, and the cooked bacon. Then season with salt and pepper (to taste), and let the soup simmer for 5 more minutes.
7. Garnish with chopped green onions and enjoy this cheesy, creamy and delicious soup!

DINNER TIME FAVORITES

FLAT IRON STEAK THAT MELTS IN YOUR MOUTH

Prep. time: 5 min

Total time: 30 min

Serves: 3-4

INGREDIENTS:

- 1 Flat Iron Steak
- Olive Oil
- 1 Tsp. Pepper
- ½ Tsp. Sea Salt
- 1 Tsp. Garlic Powder
- 1 Tsp. Onion Powder
- Butter

"I like to serve this tender, melt in your mouth steak with a large salad and loaded baked potato…. It's outstanding!"
Steve Hall

DIRECTIONS:

1. Take the Flat Iron Steak out of the refrigerator for only about 30 minutes ahead of time to allow it to come to room temperature.

2. If you buy a full-length flat iron steak cut it in half.

3. Rub it down with olive oil, and season it with a mixture of 1 tsp. pepper, 1 tsp. onion powder, 1 tsp. garlic powder, and ½ tsp. sea salt.

4. Put a thin layer of olive oil in a nonstick frying pan. Cook the steaks on high heat for 1 minute on each side.

5. Reduce heat to medium, and turn the steaks every minute (for a total of 10 to 12 times to reach medium rare or several more times to reach medium). Then add butter for more flavor the last few times you turn them.

6. Put steaks in a shallow dish, cover loosely with aluminum foil and let rest for 10 to 15 minutes. Then slice the steaks across the grain about ¼ inch thick and serve.

GRANDMA'S GREEN BEAN SLOP

INGREDIENTS:

- 1 lb. 85/15 Ground Beef
- ½ Yellow Onion (diced)
- 1 Can Green Beans French or Cut Style (drained)
- 1 Can Diced Tomatoes with Mild Green Chilies
- 1 8oz Can Tomato Sauce
- 1 Packet Taco Seasoning

Prep. time: 10 min

Total time:
20 min

Serves: 4-5

"My great Grandmother used to make this for the workers of the Pacific Railroad out west. It was easy to make in large quantities and they could scoop it up with tortillas since utensils were't always available."
Jennifer Bruce

DIRECTIONS:

1. In a skillet, on medium heat, start browning the ground beef, then add diced onions. When cooked completely, season with ½ packet of taco seasoning.

2. Then add green beans, diced tomatoes with green chilies, tomato sauce, and season with the remaining ½ packet of taco seasoning.

3. Cover with a lid and let simmer for about 10 minutes on medium heat, and it's ready.

4. Serve this on the top of lettuce for a taco salad, on chips for nachos, or just eat it with tortillas. Garnish with cheese and sour cream.

MEMPHIS STYLE BARBECUE BOLOGNA

Prep. time: 24 hours

Total time: 2 hours

Serves: 8-10

INGREDIENTS:

- 5 lb. Chub of Bologna
- 2 Tbsp. Bacon Grease
- ½ Cup Red Onion (diced)
- 1 Tbsp. Minced Garlic
- 2 Tbsp. Brown Sugar
- 1 Tbsp. Minced Ginger
- 1 Tbsp. Minced Garlic
- 1 Tbsp. Apple Cider Vinegar
- ½ Cup Ketchup
- 1 Tsp. Thyme
- ½ Bottle of Beer
- ½ Tsp. Salt
- 1 Tsp. Pepper

DIRECTIONS:

1. Make a diagonal cut around the whole 5 lb. chub of bologna about ¼ inch deep and another diagonal cut going the opposite direction. This will give you a criss-cross effect and allow the brine/marinade to soak into the bologna.
2. To make the brine/marinade, in a skillet on medium heat melt bacon grease, then sauté red onions for about 2 minutes. Then add ginger, garlic, apple cider vinegar, ketchup, brown sugar, thyme, salt, pepper, and beer. Simmer for 5 minutes and then pour mixture into a loaf pan and place the whole chub of bologna into the brine.
3. Place it in the refrigerator for 24 hours turning the chub of bologna a ¼ turn every few hours and baste with the brine/marinade.
4. Smoke the chub of bologna in a smoker for 1 ½ to 2 hours at 250 degrees basting it with the brine/marinade about every 20 minutes.
5. Slice the bologna ¼ inch thick or a bit thicker and sear the slices on the grill for 2 to 3 minutes on each side basting with the brine/marinade, or your favorite barbecue sauce.
6. Put it on a toasted bun and top it with coleslaw!
7. It can also be cubed into 1-inch squares and served with toothpicks as an appetizer.

MOM'S BEST HOMEMADE CLASSIC MEATLOAF

INGREDIENTS:

- 2 lbs. Ground Beef (85/15)
- 1 Large Onion (chopped)
- 1 Tbsp. Salt
- 1 Tsp. Black Pepper
- 1 Tbsp. Onion Powder
- 1 Tbsp. Garlic Powder
- 2 Cups Ketchup (reserve 1 cup for top of meatloaf)
- 2 ½ Tbsp. Worcestershire Sauce
- 2 Eggs
- 1 Cup Seasoned Bread Crumbs
- Nonstick Cooking Spray

Prep. time: 10 min

Total time:
60 min

Serves: 6

DIRECTIONS:

1. Preheat oven to 375 degrees.
2. In a bowl, mix all ingredients together well, but do not overmix.
3. Lightly spray a loaf pan or an 8 x 10 baking dish with nonstick cooking spray.
4. Put the meat mixture into the loaf pan or baking dish and shape into a loaf. Gently press the meat mixture into the pan and leave room around the edges of the pan for drippings. Then pour and spread the remaining 1 cup of ketchup evenly on top of the meatloaf.
5. Place in the oven and bake uncovered for about 1 hour or until meat thermometer inserted in the center of the loaf reads 160 degrees.
6. Remove meatloaf from the oven and let rest for about 20 minutes before slicing and serving. That's it, you have a classic homemade meatloaf everyone will enjoy!

DELICIOUS SWEDISH MEATBALLS

INGREDIENTS:

Meatball Ingredients:
- 1 lb. Ground Beef 85/15
- 1 lb. Ground Pork 75/25
- ½ Sweet Onion (finely chopped)
- ¼ Cup Milk
- 2 Eggs
- 1/3 Cup Plain Bread Crumbs
- 1 Tsp. Worcestershire Sauce
- ½ Tsp. Salt
- ½ Tsp. Pepper
- ½ Tsp. Allspice
- ½ Tsp. Ground Nutmeg
- ⅛ Tsp. Cayenne Pepper
- 1 Tbsp. Butter

Gravy Ingredients:
- 3 Tbsp. Butter
- 3 Tbsp. All-Purpose Flour
- 3 Cups Beef Stock or Broth
- Salt and Pepper to taste
- ¼ Cup Sour Cream
- 1 Tsp. Worcestershire Sauce
- 2 Tbsp. Heavy Whipping Cream
- ½ Tsp. Sugar

| Prep. time: 65 min | Total time: 45 min | Serves: 4 |

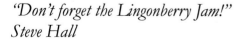

"Don't forget the Lingonberry Jam!"
Steve Hall

DIRECTIONS:

1. Preheat oven to 400 degrees.

2. In a large frying pan melt 1 tbsp. of butter on medium heat. Then add onions and sauté until soft.

3. Place onions in a bowl and add milk, eggs, plain bread crumbs, and whisk together. Then add in Worcestershire sauce, salt, pepper, allspice, ground nutmeg, cayenne pepper, and whisk that all together. Now add the ground beef and ground pork and mix well. Cover with plastic wrap and refrigerate for 1 hour.

4. Take a small scoop and form the meat into equally sized meatballs. Then, wet your hands with cold water and roll the meatballs up.

5. Put the meatballs on a foil lined cookie sheet (sprayed with nonstick cooking spray) and bake at 400 degrees for 25 to 30 minutes. While they are baking, you can make the gravy.

6. In the same frying pan you used to soften the onions, melt 3 tbsp. of butter on medium heat and add 3 tbsp. of regular flour, then cook it, whisking continuously, for about 5 minutes. or until a golden brown color. Pour in a little beef stock at a time and keep stirring until the gravy is a bit thinner than regular gravy and season with salt and pepper to taste. Then add sour cream, Worcestershire sauce, heavy cream and sugar. Simmer for 3 to 5 minutes, then turn down to low heat until the meatballs have finished baking.

7. When the meatballs are done, put them in the gravy and simmer the meatballs in the gravy for 5 to 7 minutes.

8. Serve the meatballs and gravy on a bed of egg noodles along with petite gold potatoes and a small dish of Lingonberry Jam. Drizzle butter on the taters with a dollop of sour cream and a sprinkle of dill or chives.

BAKED STUFFED CABBAGE ROLLS

INGREDIENTS:

- 1 lb. Ground Beef 85/15
- 1 Large Head of Cabbage
- 3 Tbsp. Olive Oil
- 1 Tbsp. Butter
- 1 Medium Onion (finely diced)
- 1 ½ Tbsp. Garlic (minced)
- 1 ½ Cups Mushrooms (chopped)
- ¾ Cup White Rice (uncooked)
- 4 Tbsp. Chopped Fresh Parsley (reserve 1 Tbsp. for garnish)
- 1 15oz. Can Tomato Puree
- ¾ Cup Beef Broth
- 1 ½ Tsp. Salt
- 1 Tsp. Pepper
- 1 Tsp. Garlic Powder
- 1- 2 Tbsp. Worcestershire Sauce
- ¾ Cup Diced Tomatoes

Prep. time: 25 min

Total time: 2 hours

Serves: 6

DIRECTIONS:

1. Preheat oven to 350 degrees.

2. Bring a large pot of water to a boil. Cut the center core out of the cabbage and place the core side down in boiling water. Cover and simmer for about 10 minutes or until leaves are softened. Then place the cabbage on a baking pan and carefully start removing the loose outer layers of cabbage leaves with a fork, cutting them away with a knife from the core. Place each leaf on the baking pan and cut out the thick spine with a knife so it will be easier to roll. If the inner leaves are not tender enough, you may need to put the cabbage head back into the boiling water for a few more minutes to soften them.

3. While cabbage is cooking, in a skillet on medium high heat, add olive oil and melt butter. Then add onions and sauté until they are tender. Add garlic and mushrooms and continue cooking for another 3 minutes. Remove from heat and set aside (you will be adding this to the meat mixture).

4. In a large bowl, add ground beef, cooked onion, garlic and mushroom mixture, uncooked rice, parsley, 1 cup tomato puree, Worcestershire sauce, garlic powder, salt, and pepper and combine well.

5. In a small separate bowl, mix together the remaining 1 cup tomato puree and beef broth. Pour 3 to 4 large spoonfuls of the sauce into the bottom of a 9 x 13 baking pan.

6. Divide the bowl of meat mixture into quarters. Each quarter will stuff 3 cabbage leaves for a total of 12 rolls. Fill each leaf with a spoonful of the meat mixture. Then as you are rolling them up, tuck in the sides and place them seam side down in the baking pan. Pour the remaining sauce over the cabbage rolls and spoon some diced tomatoes on top. Cover the pan tightly with foil and bake for 1 ½ hours (You may want to place the pan on a cookie sheet in case it drips).

7. Remove from the oven and let rest for 30 minutes. Garnish with fresh parsley and serve with sour cream. So delicious….your family will love this classic recipe!

CHICKEN FRIED STEAK WITH CHUCK WAGON GRAVY

Prep. time: 25 min | Total time: 45 min | Serves: 4

INGREDIENTS:

- 4 Cube Steaks or Top Sirloin (tenderized)
- 4 eggs
- 1 Tsp. Paprika
- ¾ Cup Buttermilk
- 2 ½ Cups All-Purpose Flour
- 3 Tbsp. Lemon Pepper
- 1 Tbsp. Cornstarch
- 2 Tbsp. Seasoning Salt
- All-Vegetable Shortening or Oil
- ¼ Cup Bacon Grease
- 2 Cups Whole Milk
- ¼ Tsp. Salt
- ½ Tsp. Pepper

DIRECTIONS:

1. For the steak you will need 2 shallow bowls for the wet and dry mixture you will be coating them with. In bowl #1 add eggs, paprika, buttermilk, and whisk well. In bowl #2 add flour, lemon pepper, cornstarch, seasoning salt, and mix together well (reserve ¼ cup of seasoned flour mixture to make the gravy).

2. Dip the steak in the egg mixture, then in the flour mixture. Then repeat this step one more time coating both sides, and lay them on a rack and let them rest for 15 minutes.

3. Pour ½ inch deep oil (or melt vegetable shortening) in a cast iron skillet and bring to 350 degrees.

4. Cook steaks until golden brown on both sides, then place them on a rack or paper towels. To keep the steaks warm while making the gravy, place them in a baking dish and put in the oven at 400 degrees for about 5 minutes.

5. To make the gravy, drain the oil in the skillet, but keep about 2 tablespoons of the drippings. Turn the heat to medium and add in ¼ cup bacon grease, or you can use ¼ cup of the oil left from frying the steaks. Then whisk in ¼ cup of the seasoned flour you reserved.   Cook the flour and grease on medium heat, whisking constantly for about 2 minutes. Then add whole milk a little at a time and continue whisking. Simmer for 2 to 3 more minutes. Once the gravy thickens, add salt and pepper.

6. Take the steaks out of the oven, place them on a plate, and smother them with gravy. Sprinkle just a bit of black pepper on top and serve with mashed potatoes ….and you have the absolute best comfort food ever!

CREAMY GARLIC CHICKEN AND POTATOES

INGREDIENTS:

- 6 Chicken Thighs
- 1 Tsp. Salt
- 1 Tsp. Pepper
- 1 Tsp. Garlic Salt
- 1 Tsp. Onion Powder
- 1 Tsp. Garlic Powder
- 1 Tsp. Red Pepper Flakes
- 1 Tsp. Paprika
- Olive Oil
- 1 Stick Salted Butter
- 6 Potatoes (Gold & Red Potatoes)
- 4 Cups Fresh Spinach
- 4 Tbsp. Chopped Garlic
- 2 Tbsp. Flour
- 1 Cup Chicken Broth
- ½ Cup Half and Half
- ½ Cup Heavy Cream
- ½ Cup Parmesan Cheese (grated or shredded)
- 5 Tsp. Fresh Chopped Parsley
- 5 Tsp. Fresh Chopped Basil

Prep. time: 20 min | Total time: 90 min | Serves: 4-6

DIRECTIONS:

1. Preheat oven to 400 degrees.
2. In a small bowl, mix together the garlic salt, garlic powder, onion powder, red pepper flakes, and paprika. Then sprinkle the seasoning mix on both sides of the chicken thighs.
3. Place the chicken thighs on a plate and cover them with plastic wrap. Then put them in the refrigerator for about 1 hour while preparing the potatoes, spinach, and sauce.

4. Wash and dry the potatoes, then cut each potato into 8 equal size pieces. Place the potatoes into a 9 x 13 baking dish and drizzle olive oil on them. Season with salt and pepper. Potatoes take longer to cook, so partially bake the potatoes in a 400 degree preheated oven for 30 minutes, then remove from the oven and set aside.

5. In a large skillet on medium heat, add 2 tbsp olive oil and melt 2 tbsp. butter. Then sear the chicken thighs, skin side down first, until golden brown, then flip over and sear the other side until golden brown (about 3 minutes on each side). Remove the chicken thighs from the pan and place them on a plate.

6. In the same skillet, add 1 tbsp. olive oil to the chicken drippings and sauté the spinach until wilted down a little. Remove the spinach from the pan and set aside in a separate bowl.

7. In the same skillet, melt 4 tbsp. butter and add 1 tbsp. olive oil. Then add the chopped garlic and sauté for about 1 minute, or until it gets fragrant. Add the flour (whisking continuously) and cook for about 2 minutes. Then pour in the chicken broth, and continue to whisk as the sauce cooks and thickens. Whisk in the half and half, heavy cream, parmesan cheese, freshly chopped basil and parsley, and cook for another minute.

8. Place the chicken thighs in the baking dish with the partially cooked potatoes, then add the spinach. Pour the garlic sauce over the top of the chicken thighs, potatoes, and spinach.
9. Bake at 400 degrees for 45 minutes, or until the chicken and the potatoes are fully cooked. Remove from the oven and serve. Heavenly, tender and so delicious!

CROCKPOT HONEY GARLIC CHICKEN

INGREDIENTS:

- 6 to 8 Chicken Thighs (skinless, boneless)
- ½ Cup Honey
- ¼ Cup Ketchup
- ¼ Cup Soy Sauce
- 2 to 3 Cloves Garlic (chopped)
- 1 Tsp. Oregano
- 1 Tsp. Parsley
- 6 Red Potatoes (cut into quarters)
- 2 Cups Baby Carrots
- 1 Medium Sweet Yellow Onions (sliced)
- Nonstick Cooking Spray

Prep. time:
15 min

Total time:
5-7 hours

Serves: 4

DIRECTIONS:

1. In a bowl, mix together the honey, ketchup, soy sauce, garlic, oregano, and parsley.

2. Spray a 6 quart crockpot with nonstick cooking spray. Then place the chicken thighs in the bottom and add in the potatoes, carrots, and onions. Then pour the honey garlic sauce over the top.

3. Cook on high for 5 hours, or on low for 7 hours. Then serve and enjoy!

MAMA MARGE'S CHICKEN AND DUMPLINGS

INGREDIENTS:

- 1 Whole Chicken
- 1 Can Cream of Chicken Soup
- ½ Stick Salted Butter
- 2 Cups Self-Rising Flour
- 2 Tbsp. (rounded) Vegetable Shortening
- 1 Egg
- 1 Cup Whole Milk
- Salt and Pepper to taste

Prep. time: 20 min

Total time: 65 min

Serves: 6

DIRECTIONS:

1. In a large pot on medium heat, place the whole chicken in the pot and pour in enough water to cover it. Bring to a boil and cook the chicken until tender (about 50 minutes). While the chicken is cooking, prepare the dumplings. When the chicken is fully cooked, remove the chicken from the pot and place on a plate to cool. Then remove chicken meat from the bones, shred and set aside.

2. Add 1 can of cream of chicken soup and ½ stick of butter to the chicken broth in the pot. Season with salt and pepper to taste and bring to a simmer.

3. To make the dumplings, in a bowl add the flour. Then add and cut the vegetable shortening into the flour with a pastry cutter/blender or fork. Then pour in half of the milk and 1 egg, and stir together. Pour in the rest of the milk and stir until the batter is thick and slightly sticky.

4. Pour the dumpling mixture onto wax paper dusted with some flour and knead a couple of times until the dough is smooth. Put some flour on a rolling pin and roll the dough out to about ¼ inch thick (adding flour as needed to avoid sticking). Then cut into strips with a pizza cutter (about every ¾ inches both ways) making cubes.

5. Gently drop the little cubes of dumpling dough into the boiling chicken broth and cook for about 15 minutes until they are fluffy and tender (do not stir them in the broth, just tap them down gently with a spoon).

6. Then add the shredded chicken and cook for about 5 more minutes and serve! You will love this classic homemade recipe.

MOMMA DONNA'S ONE SKILLET CHICKEN POT PIE

Prep. time: 15 min

Total time:
50 min

Serves: 4

INGREDIENTS:

- 1 Rotisserie Chicken (shredded)
- 2 Tbsp. Olive Oil
- 4 Tbsp. Salted Butter
- 1 Cup Yellow Onions (diced)
- 2 Cups Frozen Potatoes O'Brien (thawed)
- 1 Can Chicken Broth
- 1 Can Cream of Chicken Soup
- 1 12oz. bag Frozen Peas and Carrots (thawed)
- 1 Box Refrigerated Pie Crusts
- 1 Egg (beat together with 1 tsp. of water)
- Salt and Pepper to taste

DIRECTIONS:

1. Preheat oven to 400 degrees.
2. In a cast iron skillet, add olive oil and melt butter, then add diced onions and sauté until tender .
3. Add thawed Potatoes O'Brien, season with salt and pepper and cook for about 5 minutes.
4. Then add cream of chicken soup, chicken broth, peas and carrots, and shredded chicken (salt and pepper to taste). Stir and let simmer for 5 minutes. Remove from heat and let cool for about 5 minutes.
5. Unroll 1 softened pie crust (as directed on the box) and place on top of the chicken mixture (completely covering it to the inside edge of the skillet).
6. Cut 6 small slits on the top of the pie crust to create steam vents. Then with a basting brush, lightly brush the pie crust with the egg wash.
7. Bake in the oven for 40 minutes, or until golden brown. Remove from the oven and let set for about 15 minutes and serve. So easy and so delicious!

STEVE'S CRISPY FRIED CHICKEN

INGREDIENTS:

- 4 Cups Water
- ¼ Cup Salt
- ¼ Cup Sugar
- 8 - 10 Peppercorns
- 1 Slice of Lemon
- 1 Clove of Garlic
- 2 Bay Leaves

Chicken

- 1 Whole Cut up Chicken
- Vegetable Oil

Breading

- 1 Cup Bread Flour
- 1 Cup Rice Flour
- 1 Tbsp. Cornstarch
- 1 Tsp. Pepper
- ½ Tsp. Salt

Prep. time: 2-4 hrs

Total time: 50 min

Serves: 3-4

DIRECTIONS:

1. In a large pot on medium-high heat, add water, salt, sugar, peppercorns, lemon, garlic and bay leaves. Bring the brine to a boil, then put the heat on low and simmer for 1 to 2 minutes just to dissolve the salt and sugar. Then remove from heat and let it cool off (Toss in a few ice cubes to help cool it).

2. Put the chicken pieces in a container or bowl with a cover. Once the brine has cooled off, pour it over the chicken pieces (make sure all the chicken is completely covered with the brine), then cover and put in the refrigerator for 2 to 4 hours, or overnight.

3. Take the chicken out of the refrigerator and remove the chicken pieces from the brine. Then pat each chicken piece dry with paper towels. Let the chicken rest for 2 to 3 hours until it is room temperature (this will help the flour mixture to stick to the chicken and not cool down the oil in the pan when frying them).

4. In a shallow bowl, add all the dry breading ingredients and mix together. Then dredge each piece of chicken in the breading mix (shake any excess breading mix off each piece).

5. Preheat oven to 350 degrees. In a deep skillet, add vegetable oil (about 1½ inches deep) and heat it up between 300 to 325 degrees. Then fry each piece of chicken in the skillet until golden brown on both sides (only fry a few pieces of chicken at a time and don't overcrowd, and check the oil temperature between each batch). Place the golden brown chicken on a baking sheet with a rack (not paper towels).

6. Then take the chicken on the baking sheet with a rack and finish baking them in the oven at 350 degrees until all the pieces reach an internal temperature of 165 degrees.

7. Remove chicken from the oven and let it rest for about 20 to 25 minutes before serving. Best homemade fried chicken ever!

CHICKEN AND SAUSAGE GUMBO

Prep. time: 20 min | Total time: 1.5 hours | Serves: 4-6

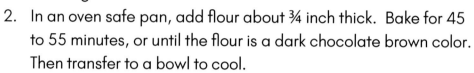

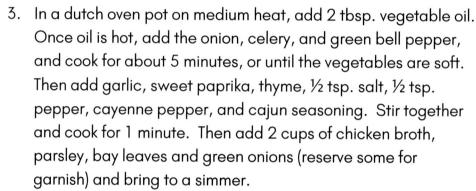

INGREDIENTS:

- 6 Chicken Thighs (skinless, boneless)
- 1 Pkg. 4 links Cajun Style Andouille Smoked Sausage
- 1 Cup All-Purpose Flour
- 4 Cups Chicken Broth
- 5 Tbsp. Vegetable Oil
- 1 Sweet Onion (diced)
- 3 Green Onions (chopped)
- 2 Stalks of Celery (diced)
- 1 Green Bell Pepper (diced)
- 1 Tbsp. Garlic
- 1 Tsp. Sweet Paprika,
- 1 Tbsp. Thyme
- 1 Tsp. Salt
- 1 Tsp. Black Pepper
- ⅛ Tsp. Cayenne Pepper
- ½ Tsp. Cajun Seasoning
- ½ Tsp. Garlic Powder
- ½ Tsp. Onion Powder
- 1 Tbsp. Parsley
- 2 Bay Leaves
- 1 Tsp White Vinegar

"Drop the spoon fantastic… outstanding!" - Steve Hall

DIRECTIONS:

1. Preheat oven to 425 degrees.
2. In an oven safe pan, add flour about ¾ inch thick. Bake for 45 to 55 minutes, or until the flour is a dark chocolate brown color. Then transfer to a bowl to cool.
3. In a dutch oven pot on medium heat, add 2 tbsp. vegetable oil. Once oil is hot, add the onion, celery, and green bell pepper, and cook for about 5 minutes, or until the vegetables are soft. Then add garlic, sweet paprika, thyme, ½ tsp. salt, ½ tsp. pepper, cayenne pepper, and cajun seasoning. Stir together and cook for 1 minute. Then add 2 cups of chicken broth, parsley, bay leaves and green onions (reserve some for garnish) and bring to a simmer.
4. In a small bowl, mix together ½ tsp. salt, ½ tsp. black pepper, garlic powder, and onion powder. Cut the chicken thighs in half and sprinkle the seasoning mixture on them.
5. In a skillet on medium heat, add 3 tbsp. vegetable oil. Once hot, place the chicken thighs in the skillet and lightly sear both sides. Then remove the chicken and add them into the dutch oven pot. Cover and simmer for 15 minutes, then take the chicken out of the pot and place them on a plate to cool. Then shred or cut into cubes, and set aside.
6. In the bowl with flour you baked earlier, slowly whisk in 2 cups of chicken broth. Whisk until the flour is completely dissolved. Then pour into the dutch oven pot.
7. Slice the sausage and add them into the dutch oven pot. Simmer for about 5 minutes.
8. Add the shredded or cubed chicken into the dutch oven pot. Then add 1 tsp. white vinegar and salt to taste.
9. Serve over a bed of white rice with a scoop of potato salad on top, and sprinkle with some chopped green onions.

SOUTHERN HOME FRIED POTATOES AND SAUSAGE

INGREDIENTS:

- 1 16oz. Pkg. Polska Kielbasa Smoked Sausage (sliced)
- 7 Tbsp. Olive Oil (or Bacon Grease)
- 1 Medium Yellow Onion (chopped)
- 1 Can Green Beans (drained)
- 5 Large Potatoes (peeled and sliced)
- 1 Tbsp. Minced Garlic
- 1 Tsp. Salt
- 1 Tsp. Pepper
- ½ Tsp. Red Pepper Flakes
- Garnish with Chives

Prep. time: 10 min

Total time:
30 min

Serves: 4

DIRECTIONS:

1. Peel and slice 5 large potatoes. (slice potatoes in half, then cut them into slices about ¼ inch thick). Put the potatoes in a bowl and coat them with 2 tbsp. olive oil. Then slice the sausage link about the same width, and set aside in a separate dish.

2. In a large skillet on medium heat, add 2 tbsp. bacon grease or olive oil. Add sliced sausage and cook until one side is browned. Then flip them over to brown the other side, and add in the chopped onions. Cook until onions are tender and sausage is browned. Then remove the sausage and onions from the skillet and place them on a plate, and set aside.

3. In the same skillet, add 1 tbsp. bacon grease or olive oil, green beans, and minced garlic. Cook for about 3 minutes, then place green beans aside with the sausage and onions.

4. In the same skillet, add 2 tbsp. bacon grease or olive oil and add the sliced potatoes. Fry the potatoes until both sides are golden brown and fork tender. Season the potatoes with salt, pepper, and red pepper.

5. Then add the sausage, onions and green beans back into the skillet with the potatoes, and cook for a couple more minutes. Garnish with chives...and it's ready to serve!

SLOW COOKER PORK CHOPS

Prep. time: 15 min | Total time: 5 hours | Serves: 4

INGREDIENTS:

- 4 Thick Cut Bone-in Pork Chops
- 1 Cup All-Purpose Flour
- 1 Tsp. Salt
- 1 Tsp. Pepper
- 1 Tsp. Garlic Powder
- 1 Tsp. Onion Powder
- 6 Tbsp. Bacon Grease
- 1 Tbsp. Minced Garlic
- 1 Medium Yellow Onion (diced)
- ½ Cup Red Wine
- 1 Package Onion Soup Mix
- 1 Package Pork Gravy Mix
- 1 Tbsp. Corn Starch
- 2 Cups Chicken Broth
- 1 Can Cream of Chicken Soup
- 4 Red Potatoes (sliced)

"This recipe is stand alone outstanding and so tender and delicious!" - Steve Hall

---

DIRECTIONS:

1. In a shallow bowl, mix together the flour, salt, pepper, garlic powder, and onion powder. Then dredge both sides of each pork chop in the flour mixture and set aside on a plate.
2. In a cast iron skillet on medium heat, add bacon grease and sear the pork chops until golden brown on both sides. Then set them aside on a plate.
3. Leave all the drippings in the skillet and add about 2 tbsp. of the seasoned flour mixture. Cook on medium heat,, whisking continuously, for 1 to 2 minutes to make a roux. Then add the minced garlic, diced onions, and pour in the red wine. Continue to whisk and cook for a couple of minutes.
4. Then add 1 cup of chicken broth, onion soup mix, and pork gravy mix, and cook for 3 to 4 minutes, whisking continuously.
5. In a small bowl, mix together ½ cup chicken broth and cornstarch and pour into the gravy mixture in the skillet. Then pour into the skillet the remaining ½ cup of chicken broth and stir in the cream of chicken soup and cook for a couple more minutes.
6. In a slow cooker, add sliced potatoes and then place the pork chops on top of them. Pour the gravy mixture over the pork chops. Cook 1 hour on high and then 4 hours on low. Serve with your favorite veggies and mashed potatoes!

MAINE LOBSTER ROLLS AND SWEET CORN

Prep. time: 15 min | Total time: 80 min | Serves: 2-3

INGREDIENTS:

- 2 5oz. Lobster Tails
- 3 Ears Sweet Corn (husks and silk removed)
- 1 Tsp. Salt
- 1 Tbsp. Sugar
- 3 Tbsp. Seafood Seasoning (divided)
- ½ Cup Half and Half
- 1 Tsp. Mayonnaise
- ½ Tsp. Dijon Mustard
- 1 Tsp. Finely Chopped Celery
- 1 Tsp. Finely Chopped Green Onions
- 1 Stick Butter (melted)
- 1 Tsp. Olive Oil
- 1 Tbsp. Minced Garlic or Garlic Paste
- Sub Style Bread Rolls
- Dash of Dill Weed

DIRECTIONS:

1. Fill a large pot about ¾ full of water and bring to a boil. Put the lobster tails in the boiling water with 1 tsp. salt, reduce heat and simmer for 3 to 5 minutes. Then take them out of the pot and place them in a bowl of ice water for 2 to 3 minutes. Place the lobster tails on a cutting board, then take the lobster meat out of the shell and cut into small bite size pieces. Put the lobster meat pieces in a bowl and set aside.

2. In the same pot and water used to cook the lobster tails, stir in 2 tbsp. seafood seasoning, sugar, and half and half. Bring water to a boil and gently place the ears of sweet corn in the pot and cook for 6 to 8 minutes.

3. In a small bowl, mix together Dijon mustard, celery, green onions, and a pinch of seafood seasoning. Mix in the lobster meat and chill in the refrigerator for 1 hour.

4. In a small bowl, stir together ¼ stick of melted butter, olive oil and garlic. Take two sub style rolls and slice the sides off. Then brush the sides of the rolls with the melted butter, olive oil and garlic. Place them on a medium hot skillet and cook the buttered sides of the rolls until golden brown.

5. Then remove the rolls from the skillet and cut a slice down the top making a pocket for the filling. Stuff with the chilled lobster meat, and sprinkle with a dash of dill.

6. In a shallow bowl, mix together ¾ stick of melted butter and 1 tbsp. seafood seasoning. Then roll the sweet corn in it. Serve with the delicious Maine Lobster Rolls and enjoy!

CHEESY SHRIMP AND GRITS

INGREDIENTS:

- 1 lb. Large Raw Shrimp
- 1 32oz. Box Seafood Stock
- 1 Tsp. Seafood Seasoning
- 4 Strips Bacon (diced)
- 3 Tbsp. Butter (divided)
- 2 Tbsp. All-Purpose Flour
- 1 Cup Diced Sweet Onions
- 1 Cup Diced Bell Pepper
- ½ Cup Finely Diced Celery
- 4 Drops of Balsamic Vinegar
- 4 Drops of Worcestershire Sauce
- ¼ Cup Half and Half
- ¼ Tsp. Salt
- ½ Tsp. Pepper
- ½ Tsp. Capers
- 3 Sprigs Rosemary
- 3 Lemon Slices
- ½ Tsp. Kitchen Bouquet

Grits:

- ½ Cup Half and Half
- ½ Cup Seafood Stock
- ¼ Stick Butter
- 1 Cup Instant Cheesy Grits
- ½ Cup Shredded Mild Cheddar Cheese
- 1 Tbsp. Minced Garlic

Prep. time: 15 min   Total time: 30 min   Serves: 6

1. Peel (set the shells aside in a bowl), devein, and remove the tail on the raw shrimp. Then place the shrimp in a bowl and season with seafood seasoning, and set aside.

2. In a small stock pot on medium heat, pour in the seafood stock and add the shells removed from the raw shrimp. Bring to a simmer for 5 minutes, then turn the heat off and remove/discard the shells, and set the pot of seafood stock aside.

3. In a large cast iron skillet on medium heat, cook diced bacon until crisp. Then remove the bacon with a slotted spoon and transfer to a plate lined with paper towels. Leave the bacon grease in the skillet.

4. In the skillet with the bacon grease, add butter. Once the butter has melted, add flour and whisk continuously on medium heat for 5 minutes until flour is golden brown. Then add onions, bell peppers, and celery. Cook for 3 to 5 minutes, or until the vegetables are tender.

5. Pour in 2 cups of the seafood stock (reserve ½ cup seafood stock for the grits). Then add balsamic vinegar and Worcestershire sauce and simmer for 3 minutes.

6. Pour in ¼ cup half and half, and add 2 tbsp. butter, salt, pepper, capers, rosemary, and lemon slices. Bring to a simmer for 3 to 5 minutes, then remove the rosemary and lemon slices. Stir in the kitchen bouquet and turn the heat off.

7. Prepare the grits. In a saucepan on medium heat, add 1 cup of water, ½ cup half and half, ½ cup of the seafood stock, ¼ stick of butter, and a pinch of salt and black pepper. Bring to a boil, then slowly add instant cheesy grits and stir for 1 minute on medium heat. Then add cheddar cheese and continue to cook and stir for 1 minute. Remove from heat and set aside.

8. In the cast iron skillet with the seafood stock and vegetables, turn heat on medium and add shrimp and minced garlic. Cook about 5 minutes, or until shrimp turns pink.

9. Pour the shrimp mixture over a bowl of those cheesy grits and garnish with crumbled bacon and some sliced green onions!

FISH AND CORN FRITTERS

Prep. time: 15 min | Total time: 45 min | Serves: 4

INGREDIENTS:

- 5 Tilapia Fillets
- 1 Can Sweet Corn (drained)
- ½ Cup Green Onions (chopped)
- ¼ Tsp. Cumin
- 1 Tsp. Coriander
- 1 Tbsp. Minced Garlic
- 2 Eggs (lightly beaten)
- 1 Tbsp. (heaping) Yellow Corn Meal
- ¼ Cup Cornstarch
- ½ Cup All-Purpose Flour
- ¼ Tsp. Salt
- ¼ Tsp. Pepper
- ⅓ Cup Finely Chopped Celery
- ¼ Cup Cilantro (or a bit less)
- 1 Tsp. Sugar (optional)
- Canola Oil

Dipping sauce:
- ¾ Cup Dijon Mustard
- ¼ Cup Pure Maple Syrup

DIRECTIONS:

1. Preheat oven to 350 degrees.
2. Place Tilapia on a baking pan sprayed with nonstick cooking spray, and bake in the oven for about 20 minutes, or until fork tender.
3. Remove from the oven and let cool. Then flake the Tilapia with a fork (should make about 2 cups of flaked fish).
4. In a large bowl, add and mix together the flaked Tilapia, sweet corn, green onions, cumin, coriander, and garlic. Then stir in the eggs, yellow corn meal, cornstarch, and flour. Add salt, pepper, celery, sugar (optional), and cilantro. Mix all ingredients together until well combined.
5. Form into small patties about 5/8 inch thick.
6. Fry in a deep skillet with canola oil at 360 degree until golden brown. Remove and place on a serving plate lined with paper towels.
7. In a small bowl, mix together the dipping sauce ingredients. Then serve on a platter with the fritters and enjoy.

SHRIMP EGG FOO YOUNG

Prep. time: 15 min | Total time: 45 min | Serves: 4

INGREDIENTS:

Gravy:
- ¼ Cup Cornstarch
- ¼ Cup Cold Water
- 1½ Cups Chicken Broth
- ½ Tsp. Pure Sesame Oil
- 1 Tbsp. Soy Sauce
- 2 Tbsp. Oyster Sauce
- ½ Tsp. Sugar
- Dash of Black Pepper

Vegetables:
- 2 Tbsp. Vegetable Oil
- ¼ Cup Mixed Red and Yellow Onions (diced)
- 1 Cup Mushrooms (sliced)
- 1 Cup Mixed Green and Red Bell Peppers (diced)
- 1 Cup Bean Sprouts
- Salt and Pepper

Shrimp:
- 1 Cup Small Cooked Shrimp (peeled, deveined, no tail)
- 1 Cup Frozen Peas and Carrots (thawed)
- 8 Eggs (lightly beaten)
- ¼ Cup Vegetable Oil
- Garnish with Sliced Green Onion

DIRECTIONS:

1. In a pot on medium heat, add chicken broth, sesame oil, soy sauce, oyster sauce and sugar. Stir together and bring to a low boil. In a small bowl, stir together cornstarch and water until smooth. Then slowly pour the cornstarch slurry into the pot and stir until the gravy thickens. Turn the heat down to low to keep warm.

2. In a wok or skillet on medium heat, add 2 tbsp. vegetable oil. Cook the red and yellow onions, mushrooms, green and red bell peppers for about 3 to 4 minutes, then add the bean sprouts and continue to cook until the vegetables are tender. Season with salt and pepper, remove them from the wok and put them in a large bowl Then add the cooked shrimp, peas and carrots (thawed), and eggs. Mix together until combined.

3. Heat about ⅛ cup vegetable oil in the wok on medium heat. Then scoop about ½ cup of the egg mixture into the wok. Fry until the egg is cooked and both sides are golden brown. Then place the patty on a plate lined with paper towels and pat the top of the patty with a paper towel. Repeat with the remaining egg mixture.

4. Place the egg patties on a plate or serving platter and spoon the gravy over them. Garnish with sliced green onions and salt and pepper to taste.

PASTA AND PIZZA

FABULOUS PIZZA WITH 2 INGREDIENT PIZZA DOUGH

Prep. time: 20 min

Total time: 25 min

Serves: 4-5

INGREDIENTS:

Pizza Dough:
- 1½ Cups Self-Rising Flour
- 1 Cup Plain Greek Yogurt
(Makes 12 inch pizza)
- 3 Cups Self-Rising Flour
- 2 Cups Plain Greek Yogurt
(Makes 16 inch pizza)

Pizza Toppings:
- 1 Jar Pizza Sauce
- 3 Cups Shredded Mozzarella Cheese
- 1 Medium Yellow Onion (chopped)
- 1 Cup Sliced Mushrooms
- 1 8oz. Pkg. Sliced Pepperoni
- 1 8oz. Pkg. Sliced Canadian Bacon (sliced into quarters)
- 1 20oz. Can Pineapple Tidbits in 100% Pineapple Juice (well drained)
- 2 Tbsp. Olive Oil
- Nonstick Cooking Spray

"A famous cook once said, "Pineapple should be illegal on pizza." but I say you just have to give it a try, it's absolutely phenomenal." Steve Hall

DIRECTIONS:

1. Preheat oven to 450 degrees.
2. Pour the self-rising flour into the bowl of a stand mixer with a dough hook attachment. Turn the mixer on low and slowly add in the greek yogurt. Let it kneed for about 3 to 5 minutes, or until the dough forms into a ball. If the dough is sticky, add a pinch of self-rising flour, a little at a time, until it forms into a ball. Then take the dough out of the stand mixer bowl, sprinkle with a little bit of self-rising flour and form into a ball. Place the dough ball in a bowl, cover with plastic wrap, and set aside for about 15 minutes to rise.
3. In a pan on medium heat, add olive oil and cook onions and mushrooms until tender. Then remove from heat and set aside.Spray a pizza baking pan with nonstick cooking spray. Then place the dough ball on the pan. Shape and spread it out with your hands leaving a small ridge around the edge.
4. Pour pizza sauce on the dough and spread evenly with a spoon up to the small ridge around the edge, and sprinkle with 1 cup of the mozzarella cheese. Then on half of the pizza, add the onions, mushrooms and pepperoni slices, and the other half add the pineapple and Canadian bacon. Sprinkle the entire pizza with the remaining 2 cups of the mozzarella cheese. Then on half of the pizza top with more pepperoni slices and the other half top with more Canadian bacon.
5. Bake for about 25 minutes, or until the cheese is melted and the pizza crust is golden brown. Then let it cool, slice and serve!

MOMMA DONNA'S MEAT SAUCE LASAGNA

INGREDIENTS:

- 2 lbs. Lasagna Noodles
- 1 lb. 85/15 Ground Beef
- 1 lb. Italian Sausage (mild)
- 1 Yellow Onion (chopped)
- 2 Tbsp. Chopped Garlic
- 2 24oz. Jars Marinara Sauce
- 2 24oz. Jars Tomato Basil Sauce
- 4 Tbsp. Fresh Basil
- 1 Tsp. Red Pepper Flakes
- Salt, Pepper and Garlic Salt (season to taste)
- 1 Tbsp. Sugar

Ricotta Cheese Mixture:
- 2 32oz. Tubs Ricotta Cheese
- 1 Egg
- 2 Cups Grated Parmesan Cheese
- 2 Cups Shredded Parmesan Cheese
- 4 Cups Shredded Mozzarella Cheese
- 4 Tbsp. Fresh Parsley
- 1 Tsp. Pepper

Other Ingredients and Items:
- Olive Oil or Nonstick Cooking Spray (to grease baking dish)
- Foil and Parchment Paper

Prep. time: 20 min | Total time: 90 min | Serves: 6

DIRECTIONS:

1. Preheat oven to 375.
2. In a large saucepan on medium heat, brown the ground beef and Italian sausage (remove the casing from Italian sausage and break it up with a spoon along with ground beef). Add chopped onions, and garlic, then season with salt, pepper and a little garlic salt.
3. Pour in jars of marinara sauce and tomato basil sauce, and add basil, red pepper, and sugar. Reduce heat to low, partially cover and let simmer while cooking the lasagna noodles.

4. In a 5 qt. stock pot bring water to a gentle boil on medium heat, then add about 1 tbsp. of salt and lasagna noodles. Only cook lasagna noodles about 6 min. or until al dente. Drain and rinse the lasagna noodles with cold water and drain again. Then set aside.

5. In a large bowl, mix the ricotta cheese, egg, 1 cup grated parmesan cheese, parsley. and pepper. Grease a large deep dish casserole dish with olive oil or spray with nonstick cooking spray. Add about 1 cup of the meat sauce and spread it thinly on the bottom of the casserole dish. Then add the first layer of lasagna noodles (slightly overlapping them).

6. Spread ½ of the ricotta cheese mixture evenly over the lasagna noodles, then add about 1½ cups of meat sauce over the ricotta cheese mixture and spread it evenly with a spoon. Then add a layer of mozzarella cheese and parmesan cheese. Make another layer starting with lasagna noodles, then ricotta cheese mixture, then meat sauce, and mozzarella cheese and parmesan cheese. Finish with a layer of lasagna noodles, then more meat sauce, and top with remainder of mozzarella cheese and parmesan cheese.

7. Cover with a sheet of parchment paper first, then a sheet of foil. Bake at 375 degrees for 40 minutes, then remove foil and parchment paper and bake for another 20 minutes, or until cheese is melted, bubbling, and golden brown around the edges.

8. Remove from the oven and let rest for about 20 minutes before slicing and serving.

GROUND BEEF STROGANOFF

Prep. time:
20 min

Total time:
30 min

Serves: 5-6

INGREDIENTS:

- 2 lbs. Ground Beef (80/20)
- ½ Tsp. Garlic Powder
- ½ Tsp. Onion Powder
- 1 Stick of Butter
- 2 Medium Yellow Onions (diced)
- 3 Cups Mushrooms (sliced in half)
- 1 10.5oz. Can Beef Consommé
- ⅓ Cup All-Purpose Flour
- ⅓ Cup Water
- 1 Tsp. Minced Garlic
- 1½ Cups Sour Cream
- 1 Tbsp. Tomato Paste
- 1 16oz. Bag Extra Wide Egg Noodles
- 1 Tsp. Olive Oil
- Salt
- Pepper
- Parsley Flakes

DIRECTIONS:

1. In a skillet on medium heat, brown the ground beef. Then season with ¼ tsp. of salt, pepper, garlic powder, and onion powder (½ tsp. of each). Pour the ground beef into a colander with a glass bowl under it to drain the fat, then set aside.

2. In the same skillet on medium heat, add ½ stick of butter. When the butter has melted, add diced onions and cook until soft. Then add the other ½ stick of butter and sliced mushrooms. Continue to cook until the mushrooms are tender. Sprinkle with a little salt and pepper, then transfer the onions and mushrooms into a bowl and set aside.

3. In a small bowl, add all-purpose flour and water in equal parts and stir together until smooth to make a slurry, then set aside.

4. In the same skillet on medium heat, pour in the can of beef consommé (do not dilute with water). Then slowly stir in the slurry and cook for about 3 to 4 minutes (continue to stir while it is cooking).

5. Add minced garlic, sour cream and tomato paste and salt and pepper to taste. then let simmer for a few minutes.

6. Reduce heat to low and add the cooked mushrooms, onions, and ground beef into the beef consommé mixture. Let it simmer while the egg noodles are cooking.

7. Cook the egg noodles according to package directions and drain. Then gently stir in a teaspoon of olive oil in the drained egg noodles to keep them from sticking together.

8. Lay a bed of the hot egg noodles in a serving dish and spoon some of the ground beef mixture on top of the egg noodles.

CLASSIC HOMEMADE GOULASH

INGREDIENTS:

- 2 lbs. Ground Beef (80/20)
- 2 Tbsp. Olive Oil
- 1 Large Sweet Onion (diced)
- 1 Green Bell Pepper (diced)
- 1 14.5oz. Can Diced Tomatoes (with basil, garlic, oregano)
- 1 14.5oz. Can Stewed Tomatoes
- 1 24oz. Jar Pasta Sauce
- 1 Tbsp. Italian Seasoning
- 1 Tbsp. Paprika
- 1 Tbsp. Minced Garlic
- 1 Tbsp. Chopped Basil
- 1 Tsp. Chili Powder
- 1 Tsp. Soy Sauce
- 1 Tsp. Worcestershire Sauce
- 3 Cups Beef Broth
- 2 Bay Leaves
- 1 Tsp. Sugar
- 1 16oz. Box Large Elbow Macaroni
- Salt and Pepper

"This recipe brings back so many great memories...hope it does for you too!"
Steve Hall

DIRECTIONS:

1. In a large Dutch oven on medium heat, add olive oil and cook the ground beef until it is browned. Then season with salt and pepper. Add onions and bell peppers, and cook until they are soft.
2. Then pour in the diced tomatoes, stewed tomatoes, and pasta sauce. Season with Italian seasoning, paprika, minced garlic, basil, chili powder, and sugar.
3. Add in soy sauce, Worcestershire sauce, beef broth, and bay leaves. Cover and let simmer for about 25 minutes.
4. Add in the large elbow macaroni and stir well. Then cover and let simmer for about 25 minutes (stirring occasionally) until elbow macaroni is tender.
5. Salt and pepper to taste, and serve with slices of buttered white bread!

Prep. time: 15 min

Total time: 50 min

Serves: 4

BAKED SEAFOOD MAC AND CHEESE

INGREDIENTS:

- 1 16oz. Box Penne Pasta or Large Elbow Macaroni
- 2 Tbsp. Seafood Seasoning
- 1 Tbsp. Butter
- 4 Tbsp. Olive Oil
- 4 Cups Whole Milk
- 1 Cup Heavy Whipping Cream
- ½ Cup Chopped Onion
- 1 ½ Tbsp. Minced Garlic
- 3 Tbsp. All-Purpose Flour
- 2 Cups Aged Gouda Cheese (grated)
- 3 Cups Sharp Cheddar Cheese (grated)
- 1 Cup Havarti Cheese (grated)
- 1 Cup Gruyere Cheese (grated)
- 1 lb. Shrimp (raw, deveined, tail removed, medium size)
- ¾ lb. Lobster (raw or pre-cooked)
- ¾ lb. Lump Crab or Imitation Crab
- Nonstick Cooking Spray or Butter
- Salt and Pepper to taste

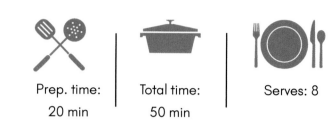

Prep. time: 20 min | Total time: 50 min | Serves: 8

DIRECTIONS:

1. Preheat oven to 350 degrees.
2. Bring a large stock pot filled ¾ full of water to a boil on medium heat. Add pasta and 2 tsp of salt, and cook (stirring occasionally) until pasta is almost done (about 3 minutes short of suggested cooking time). Then drain the pasta, but do not rinse. Gently stir in 2 tbsp. of olive oil to keep the pasta from sticking together, and set aside.
3. In a microwave safe bowl, slightly warm the milk and heavy whipping cream in the microwave for about 3 minutes.

4. In a large skillet on medium heat, add 2 tbsp. of olive oil and butter. When the butter is melted, add the onions and sauté for about 3 to 4 minutes or until soft. Then add in the flour and cook for about 1 to 2 minutes stirring continuously. Then add in the chopped garlic and cook for another minute.

5. Pour the warm milk and heavy whipping cream into the roux mixture in the skillet and continue whisking vigorously until the sauce is smooth. Once the sauce is smooth, turn the heat down to medium-low. Then add in seafood seasoning and salt and pepper. Let simmer (stirring occasionally) for about 5 to 8 minutes, or until the sauce has thickened.

6. In a large bowl, mix all 4 cheeses together, then add 3 cups of the cheese mixture into the sauce (reserve the remaining 4 cups of cheese mixture for layering). Stir until the cheese melts, then remove from heat and stir in the drained pasta.

7. In a 9 x 13 baking dish sprayed with nonstick cooking spray, pour half of the macaroni and cheese into the bottom of the baking dish, then add the first layer of shrimp, lobster, and crab, then sprinkle with 2 cups of the cheese mixture.

8. Pour in the remaining half of the macaroni and cheese, then the final layer of shrimp, lobster and crab. Season with a little of the seafood seasoning, then top with the remaining 2 cups of the cheese mixture.

9. Cover with parchment paper, then aluminum foil on top, and bake for 30 minutes and serve.

HOMEMADE SPAGHETTI AND MEATBALLS

INGREDIENTS:

- 1 12oz. Box Spaghetti
- Grated Parmesan Cheese

Meatballs:

- ¾ lb. Ground Beef (80/20)
- ½ Cup Italian Seasoned Bread Crumbs
- ⅓ Cup Whole Milk
- 1 Egg (lightly beaten)
- 1 Tsp. Minced Garlic
- ¼ Tsp. Red Pepper Flakes
- 1 Tbsp. Grated Parmesan Cheese
- ½ Tsp. Italian Seasoning
- 1 Tsp. Olive Oil
- ¼ Tsp. Salt
- ½ Tsp. Black Pepper

Sauce:

- ¼ lb. Ground Beef (80/20)
- ¼ lb. Breakfast Sausage
- 1 15oz. Can Diced Tomatoes
- 1 Small Can Tomato Paste
- 1 28oz. Can Whole Peeled Plum Tomatoes
- ½ Cup Green or Red Bell Peppers (diced)
- ½ Onion (diced)
- ½ Cup Mushrooms (diced)
- 1 Tsp. Italian Seasoning
- 2 Tsp. Sugar
- ¼ Tsp. Salt
- ½ Tsp. Pepper
- 1 Tbsp. Minced Garlic
- 1 Tsp. Oregano
- ½ Tbsp. Basil

Prep. time: 20 min | Total time: 45 min | Serves: 4-5

DIRECTIONS:

1. To make the sauce, in a large stock pot on medium heat, brown ¼ lb. ground beef and ¼ lb. breakfast sausage. Then add bell peppers, onions, and mushrooms, and cook about 3 to 4 more minutes.

2. Pour the can of whole peeled plum tomatoes into a blender and blend for a few seconds, just enough to rough chop the tomatoes. Then pour them into the large stock pot with the meat and vegetables and bring to a boil.

3. Reduce heat to medium-low and add Italian seasoning, sugar, salt, pepper, minced garlic, oregano, basil, and tomato paste. Reduce the heat to low and let it simmer.

4. To make the meatballs, in a bowl, add ¾ lb. ground beef, seasoned bread crumbs, milk, egg, garlic, salt, pepper, red pepper flakes, grated parmesan cheese, and Italian seasoning. Mix together until combined, then form into about 8 to 10 meatballs.

5. In a skillet on medium heat with about 1 tsp. olive oil, add meatballs and sear them until browned on all sides. Then add the meatballs into the stock pot with the sauce and let simmer for about 25 minutes

6. Boil spaghetti in a large stock pot with 2 tsp. of salt and cook according to package directions, then drain. Add a couple of spoonfuls of sauce and lightly toss to coat the spaghetti.

7. Serve spaghetti in a bowl, or on a dinner plate, and spoon on more of the delicious sauce and top with meatballs. Sprinkle with parmesan cheese and you are ready to eat and enjoy!

SALADS, SAUCES AND DRESSINGS

ITALIAN SPAGHETTI PASTA SALAD

INGREDIENTS:

- 1 lb. Box Thin Spaghetti
- 1 Tbsp. Kosher Salt
- 2 Tbsp. Olive Oil
- 2 Cucumbers (diced)
- 1 10oz. Package Cherry or Grape Tomatoes (sliced in half)
- 1 Small Red Onion (finely diced)
- 1 4oz. Can Sliced Black Olives (drained)
- 1 Red Bell Pepper (diced)
- 1 5oz. Bag Pepperoni Minis
- ½ Cup Grated Parmesan Cheese

Salad Dressing:
- 1 Tsp. Black Pepper
- 2 Tbsp. Italian Seasoning
- 1 Tbsp. Sugar
- 1 Tsp. Kosher Salt
- 1 Tsp. Minced Garlic
- ½ Cup Red Wine Vinegar
- 1 Cup Virgin Olive Oil

Prep. time: 10 min Total time: 60 min Serves: 4

DIRECTIONS:

1. Fill a large stock pot with water and bring to a boil on medium heat. Then add 1 tbsp. kosher salt and the spaghetti, and cook according to package directions, or until tender. Drain the spaghetti and transfer into a large bowl, then gently stir in 2 tbsp. olive oil to coat the spaghetti. Place the spaghetti in the refrigerator to chill for about 1 hour.
2. Once the spaghetti is chilled, add cucumbers, cherry tomatoes, red onions, black olives, red bell peppers, the pepperoni minis, and toss together well.
3. In a pint mason jar with a lid, add all the salad dressing ingredients together and shake well. Pour over spaghetti salad and toss to coat.
4. Chill in the refrigeration for about 4 hours, or overnight.
5. Serve with a sprinkle of parmesan cheese and a pinch of black pepper!

MISS SHEILA'S OUTSTANDING GRAPE SALAD

INGREDIENTS:

- 2 Cups Green Seedless Grapes
- 2 Cups Red Seedless Grapes
- 1 8oz. Package Cream Cheese (softened)
- 1 Cup Light Brown Sugar
- 1 Cup Chopped Pecans
- 1 Tbsp. Vanilla Extract

Prep. time: 10 min

Total time: 30 min

Serves: 8

DIRECTIONS:

1. In a large bowl, add softened cream cheese, brown sugar, chopped pecans, and vanilla extract, and mix together well.
2. Then add in the green and red grapes, and gently mix until the grapes are coated with the cream cheese mixture.
3. Chill for 30 minutes and serve.

CUCUMBER, ONION, AND TOMATO SALAD

Salad Dressing:
- ½ Cup Cold Water
- ½ Cup Apple Cider Vinegar
- ¼ Cup Extra Virgin Olive Oil
- 1 Tsp. Salt
- 1 Tsp. Black Pepper
- 2 Tbsp. Sugar

Prep. time: 15 min

Total time: 2-4 hours

Serves: 6

INGREDIENTS:

- 3 Cucumbers (peeled leaving strips of green, and sliced)
- 1 Sweet Vidalia Onion (cut in half and thinly sliced)
- 1½ Cups Cherry Tomatoes (cut in half)
- 1 Tbsp. Finely Chopped Fresh Dill

DIRECTIONS:

1. In a large mixing bowl, add cucumbers, onions, cherry tomatoes and finely chopped dill.
2. In a separate bowl, add water, apple cider vinegar, olive oil, sugar, salt and pepper. Mix together well, then pour over salad and toss until everything is coated well.
3. Chill in the refrigerator for 2 to 4 hours. Serve and enjoy!

STEVE'S FAMOUS COLESLAW

INGREDIENTS:

- 3½ Cups Cabbage (chopped thin or pre-packaged coleslaw mix)
- 1 Carrot (grated)
- 1 Cup Cherry Tomatoes (cut in half)

Coleslaw Dressing:
- 2 Cups Mayonnaise
- ½ Cup Sweet Vidalia Onions (finely diced)
- 1 Tbsp. Apple Cider Vinegar
- ½ Cup Sugar
- Pinch of Salt
- 1 Tsp. Pepper (or more to taste)

Prep. time: 15 min

Total time: 60 min

Serves: 6

DIRECTIONS:

1. In a large bowl, add cabbage, carrots, and cherry tomatoes, then set aside.
2. In a separate bowl, add mayonnaise, onions, apple cider vinegar, sugar, salt, and pepper, and whisk together until smooth and creamy.
3. Pour the coleslaw dressing over the cabbage mixture, and toss together until everything is evenly coated.
4. Cover with plastic wrap and chill in the refrigerator for an hour or more, then serve!

THE BEST BLUE CHEESE DRESSING

INGREDIENTS:

- 1½ Cups Mayonnaise
- ¼ Cup Heavy Whipping Cream
- ⅛ Tsp. Apple Cider Vinegar
- ½ Tsp. Sugar
- ½ Tsp. Mustard
- 1 Cup Crumbled Blue Cheese
- Pinch of Salt
- ½ Tsp. Pepper

DIRECTIONS:

1. In a bowl, add all ingredients, and blend together with an electric hand mixer until creamy and smooth. If you like a chunky blue cheese dressing, reserve a little of the crumbled blue cheese and stir it into the dressing after well blended with the electric hand mixer.
2. Pour into a glass mason jar, cover and chill in the refrigerator. Then serve with your favorite salad, buffalo wings, steak or hamburger....it is the Best Ever!

"I gotta give credit where credit is due...I got this recipe from my sister-in-law, Eyvonne, up there in Brainerd, Mn...the first time I ate it, I flipped out and had her give me the recipe...I absolutely love it!" - Steve Hall

RED'S CRAB LOUIE SALAD

INGREDIENTS:

Salad Dressing:
- ½ Cup Mayonnaise
- ⅓ Cup Ketchup
- 1 Tbsp. Sweet Pickle Relish
- 1 Tbsp. Finely Chopped Black Olives
- 1 Tbsp. Finely Chopped Green Bell Pepper
- 2 Hard Boiled Eggs (peeled and chopped)
- 1 Tbsp. Mayonnaise
- Salt and Pepper

Salad:
- 6 Romaine Lettuce Leaves
- 1 Head Iceberg Lettuce (finely chopped)
- 2 Roma Tomatoes (sliced lengthwise)
- 2 Avocados (sliced lengthwise)
- 1 Cucumber (peeled and sliced)
- 3 Hard Boiled Eggs (sliced in half lengthwise)
- 1 8oz. Package Imitation Crab Meat (flake style)
- 1 8oz. Package Imitation Crab Meat (chunk style)
- Fresh Dill (chopped)
- Salt and Pepper

Prep. time:
15 min

Serves: 4

DIRECTIONS:

1. Make the salad dressing. In a bowl, add 2 chopped hard boiled eggs with 1 tbsp. mayonnaise, and mix together well. Then add ½ cup mayonnaise, ketchup, sweet pickle relish, black olives, and green bell peppers, and stir together until well blended. Sprinkle it with a little salt and pepper, and put in the refrigerator to chill.

2. On a large serving platter or plate, add a layer of romaine lettuce leaves. Then add the finely chopped iceberg lettuce on top of the romaine lettuce leaves. Then place around the edge of the platter the sliced tomatoes, sliced avocados, and 3 hard boiled eggs sliced in half, and set aside.

3. In a bowl, add 8 oz. package of "flake style" imitation crab with 2 tsp. of the salad dressing, and mix together and set aside.

4. Add a couple spoonfuls of salad dressing on top of the chopped iceberg lettuce on the platter, and then add the "flake style" imitation crab mixture.

5. In a bowl, add ½ package of the "chunk style" imitation crab (reserving the other ½ of the package) and mix together with about 1 tsp. of the salad dressing. Then spoon it on top of the "flake style" crab mixture on the platter. Top with the other ½ package of "chunk style" imitation crab that was reserved.

6. Add spoonfuls of salad dressing around the outside edge of the salad. Sprinkle everything with a little salt and pepper to taste. Then garnish with some fresh dill and serve!

STEVE'S SECRET BARBECUE SAUCE

INGREDIENTS:

- 2 Cups Ketchup
- 1 Can Diced Tomatoes with Mild Green Chilies (drained)
- 1 Small Can Anchovies (only need 3 Anchovies for the sauce)
- ½ Cup Molasses
- ½ Cup Brown Sugar
- ¼ Cup Orange Juice
- ¼ Cup Honey
- ¼ Cup Apple Cider Vinegar
- ¼ Cup Apple Juice
- 1 Tsp. Dry Mustard
- 1 Tsp. Garlic Powder
- 1 Tsp. Onion Powder
- 2 Tsp. Black Pepper
- ¼ Cup Grape Jelly
- ½ Cup Yellow Onion (finely diced)
- 1 Tsp. Worcestershire Sauce
- ⅛ Tsp. Cayenne Pepper (optional)
- ¼ Tsp. Liquid Smoke (optional)

| Prep. time: 10 min | Total time: 1-2 hours | Serves: 8 |

DIRECTIONS:

1. Pour the can of diced tomatoes with green chilies (drained) into a blender and blend for about 1 minute. Then add 3 anchovies and blend for another minute, or until smooth.

2. In a saucepan on medium heat, add ketchup, and the tomato mixture. Stir until blended and bring to a simmer. Then turn the heat down to low heat, and add the rest of the ingredients. Let simmer on low heat for 1 to 2 hours stirring frequently until it cooks down. Then remove from heat and let cool (sauce will thicken as it cools).

3. Pour the sauce into a mason jar and store it in the refrigerator.

HOMEMADE RANCH DRESSING

INGREDIENTS:

- 1 Cup Mayonnaise
- ½ Cup Sour Cream
- ¼ Cup Buttermilk
- ½ Tsp. Garlic Powder
- ½ Tsp. Onion Powder
- ½ Tsp. Dried Dill Weed
- ½ Tsp. Dried Chives
- ½ Tsp. Dried Parsley
- ½ Tsp. Dried Tarragon
- ¼ Tsp. Black Pepper
- Pinch of Salt
- ⅛ Tsp. Cayenne Pepper
- 2 Drops Worcestershire Sauce

DIRECTIONS:

1. In a medium bowl, add all ingredients and whisk together until well combined.
2. Pour into a mason jar with a lid and chill in the refrigerator for at least 4 hours (it is best if chilled overnight).

"Sheila just loves this stuff! She even like's to mix this with her steak sauce and dip the meat in it." -Steve Hall

VEGGIES

BAKED CABBAGE STEAKS

INGREDIENTS:

- 2 Small Heads of Cabbage
- 1 8oz. Pkg Shredded Parmesan Cheese
- 1 8oz. Pkg Shredded Mexican Blend Cheese
- Nonstick Olive Oil Cooking Spray

Sauce:
- 1 Stick Salted Butter (melted)
- 1 Tbsp. Olive Oil
- 1 Tbsp. Garlic Paste
- 1 Tsp. Black Pepper
- 1 Tsp. Smoked Paprika

Prep. time:
15 min

Total time:
45 min

Serves: 4

DIRECTIONS:

1. Preheat oven to 350 degrees.
2. Rinse and dry both heads of cabbage. Then peel off the loose green outer leaves.
3. Cut the bottom off of each cabbage head so they will sit level on the cutting board, but do not remove the core. Then cut off the 2 rounded sides on each cabbage head to square them up.
4. Slice each cabbage head into 1 inch steaks (about 4 cabbage steaks per head). Then place them on a flat baking sheet lined with aluminum foil and sprayed with nonstick olive oil cooking spray.
5. In a bowl, add the sauce ingredients, and mix together well. Then brush the sauce on top of each cabbage steak.
6. Bake uncovered in the oven for 30 minutes. Then sprinkle 4 of the steaks with parmesan cheese, and the other 4 steaks with Mexican blend cheese. Bake for another 10 to 15 minutes, or until the cheese is melted and edges are golden brown.

PERFECT FRIED GREEN TOMATOES WITH DIPPING SAUCE

INGREDIENTS:

- 4-5 Large Green Tomatoes (sliced ¼ inch thick)
- 1-2 Cups All-Purpose Flour
- 1 Tsp. Salt
- 1 Tsp. White Pepper
- 1 Tsp. Garlic Powder
- 1½ Cups Buttermilk
- 1-2 Drops Hot Sauce (Optional)
- 1 Box Plain Breadcrumbs
- Vegetable or Canola Oil

Dipping Sauce:
- ½ Cup Mayonnaise
- ½ Cup Buttermilk
- 1 Tbsp. Dill
- 1 Tsp. White Vinegar
- ½ Tsp. Salt
- ½ Tsp. Pepper
- Finely Diced Sweet Onions (Optional)

"Thank you very much to Sheila's mom, Marge, for the green tomatoes that came out of her garden!" - Steve Hall

Prep. time:
15 min

Total time:
30 min

Serves: 6

DIRECTIONS:

1. In a bowl, add the dipping sauce ingredients, and stir together until smooth and creamy. Cover with plastic wrap, and place in the refrigerator to chill while preparing the green tomatoes.

2. Slice 4 or 5 large green tomatoes, making each slice about ¼ inch thick. Then place them on a baking pan lined with paper towels. Sprinkle both sides of the tomato slices with a little salt, and set aside for about 15 minutes so they can sweat a bit.

3. Set out 3 shallow bowls. In bowl #1, add all-purpose flour seasoned with salt, white pepper and garlic powder. In bowl #2, pour in buttermilk and add 1 to 2 drops of hot sauce. In bowl #3, add bread crumbs.

4. In a cast iron skillet, pour in about ½ inch of oil, and heat to 350 degrees.

5. Then dredge each tomato slice into the bowl of seasoned flour, then dip them into the buttermilk , and then dredge in the bread crumbs.

6. Gently drop tomato slices into the cast iron skillet (don't overcrowd), and fry until golden brown on both sides. Then place them on a plate lined with paper towels to drain and cool.

7. Serve with the special dipping sauce, and enjoy this delicious classic southern recipe!

CAST IRON CORN PUDDING

INGREDIENTS:

- 4 Large Eggs
- ½ Cup Sugar
- 1 Cup Sour Cream
- 1 Tsp. Vanilla
- ⅛ Tsp. Nutmeg
- 2 Cans Cream Style Sweet Corn
- 1 12oz. Bag Frozen Golden Sweet Corn (thawed)
- 1 8.5oz. Box Corn Muffin Mix
- 1 Cup Unsalted Butter (melted and cooled)
- Nonstick Cooking Spray

Prep. time:
15 min

Total time:
50 min

Serves: 6

DIRECTIONS:

1. Preheat oven to 350 degrees.
2. In a large bowl, whisk the eggs until the whites and yolks are well blended, then add sugar, sour cream, vanilla, and nutmeg, and mix together.
3. Then stir in the cream style corn and golden sweet corn. Add corn muffin mix and the melted unsalted butter (let the butter cool down to room temperature before adding, so it doesn't cook the eggs). Fold everything together with a spatula or large spoon.
4. Spray a 12" cast iron skillet with nonstick cooking spray. Pour the corn pudding mixture into the cast iron skillet and sprinkle a little sugar on top.
5. Bake in the oven for 45 to 50 minutes, or until golden brown. Then turn the oven off and crack the door open for 15 minutes, and let it cool down a bit.
6. Remove it from the oven and let it cool down a bit more. Spread some butter on top and serve it warm.

"Because it is so good and almost like a dessert, I wanted to spray some whipped cream on top, but that might be going too far!" - Steve Hall

SWEET CORN FRITTERS

INGREDIENTS:

- 2 Cups Fresh Corn or Frozen (thawed) or Canned (drained)
- ¾ Cups All-Purpose Flour
- ¼ Cup Cornmeal
- 1½ Tsp. Baking Powder
- 1½ Tsp. Sugar
- ¼ Tsp. Salt
- 1½ Tbsp. Salted Butter (melted)
- 1 Egg (beaten)
- ½ – ¾ Cups Whole Milk
- Vegetable Oil

Prep. time:
15 min

Total time:
15 min

Serves: 6

DIRECTIONS:

1. In a bowl, whisk together flour, cornmeal, baking powder, sugar, and salt.
2. Then stir in the melted butter, egg (beat the egg first), and corn. Pour milk into the corn fritter mixture, and stir until combined (you may need to adjust the amount of milk you add depending on how thick or thin you want your batter and fritters to be).
3. Preheat a cast iron skillet on medium heat, then add just enough oil (about ¼ inch) to cover the bottom of the skillet.
4. Once the oil is hot, drop spoonfuls of the batter (to the size fritter you want) into the skillet. Cook the fritters about 3 to 4 minutes on each side until golden brown. Then place the fritters on a dish lined with paper towels. Remove any kernels of corn from the oil in the skillet before cooking the next batch, and add more oil if needed.
5. Serve hot with your choice of butter, honey, or maple syrup.

Miss Sheila likes hers in milk or just plain...you will love this old-time southern favorite....they are so delicious!

PERFECT BLOOMING ONION

INGREDIENTS:

- 1 Large Sweet Onion
- Vegetable or Canola Oil (for frying)

Batter:
- 1 Cup Milk
- 1 Cup Buttermilk
- 2 Eggs

Breading:
- 2 Cups All-Purpose Flour
- 2 Tsp. Salt
- 2 Tsp. Cayenne Pepper
- 2 Tsp. Paprika
- 1 Tsp. Black Pepper
- ½ Tsp. Oregano
- ¼ Tsp. Thyme
- ¼ Tsp. Cumin

Dipping Sauce:
- ½ Cup Mayonnaise
- 1 Tbsp. Ketchup
- 2 Tbsp. Horseradish Sauce (cream style)
- ½ Tsp. Paprika
- ¼ Tsp. Salt
- ⅛ Tsp. Oregano
- ¼ Tsp. Black Pepper
- Pinch of Cayenne Pepper

Prep. time:
20 min

Total time:
15 min

Serves: 3

DIRECTIONS:

1. In a bowl, mix together all of the dipping sauce ingredients. Place in the refrigerator while you prepare the onions.

2. In a medium bowl, add the batter ingredients, and whisk them together. Then set aside.

3. In another medium bowl, add the breading ingredients, mix together, and set aside.

4. Start with a large sweet onion. Cut ½ inch off the tip and trim the root end, then peel it. Then with a knife or onion corer, cut out the onion core (only ⅔ of the way down into the onion) and remove it.

5. Place the onion with the root side up on the cutting board, and make a cut about ½ inch away from the root and all the way down to the cutting board. Continue around the onion until you have 16 cuts evenly spaced apart. Then turn the onion over and gently spread open the pedals.

6. Dip the onion in the bowl of batter, and shake off the excess. Then put it in the bowl of breading mixture and coat well (separate the petals and sprinkle the breading mixture between them). Dip it again in the batter, and then again in the breading mixture, and place on a plate. Put it in the freezer for about 10 minutes while the oil is heating up.

7. In a large pot, add enough oil to cover the onion, but no more than ⅔ of the depth of the pot, so oil doesn't boil over when you put the onion in. Heat the oil to 350 degrees.

8. Then carefully lower the onion (petal side up) using a wire skimmer spoon into the hot oil. Cook it for about 10 minutes, or until golden brown (It will start floating after 5 minutes, but do not take it out until it is done).

9. Remove the onion from the oil and place on a plate lined with paper towels for about 5 minutes to drain. Serve on a platter with a small bowl of the dipping sauce in the middle of the onion and enjoy!

SMOKED GOUDA VEGGIE MELTS

INGREDIENTS:

- 1 Loaf French Bread
- 1 Cup Mushrooms (diced)
- 1 Cup Red Bell Pepper (diced)
- 1 Cup Sweet Onion (diced)
- 1 Cup Broccoli Florets (diced)
- 2 Tbsp. Olive Oil
- Sea Salt
- ½ Cup Mayonnaise
- 1 Tsp. Minced Garlic
- 1-2 Cups Smoked Gouda Cheese (shredded)

Prep. time:
15 min

Total time:
20 min

Serves: 6

DIRECTIONS:

1. Preheat oven to 425 degrees.
2. Slice loaf of french bread at an angle into 12 slices about ½ inch thick, then set aside.
3. Cut all the vegetables into about ¼ inch cubes. Then place them in a bowl and add olive oil, and toss until all the vegetables are coated well.
4. Pour the vegetables into a 10 x 15 baking dish, and sprinkle with a little sea salt. Roast the vegetables uncovered for about 15 minutes, or until tender (stirring them about half way through). Remove from the oven and let cool while preparing the mayonnaise mixture and french bread.
5. Place the 12 slices of french bread on a baking sheet.
6. In a small bowl, mix together the mayonnaise and minced garlic, and spread a thin layer of the mixture on top of each of the french bread slices.
7. Turn the oven on to broil. Then spoon a layer of vegetables on each of the french bread slices, and top each slice with a layer of the shredded smoked gouda cheese. Put the baking sheet on the top rack of the oven and broil for 3 to 4 minutes, or until cheese is melted and turns golden brown.

DESSERTS

MISS SHEILA'S CORNBREAD COFFEE CAKE

INGREDIENTS:

- 1½ Cups Self-Rising Flour
- 1 Cup Brown Sugar
- 1 Cup White Sugar
- 1 Cup Canola Oil
- 1 Tsp. Vanilla
- 4 Eggs (beaten)
- 1 Cup Pecans (whole or chopped)
- 1 Tsp. Honey
- Nonstick Baking Spray

Prep. time:
10 min

Total time:
35 min

Serves: 10

DIRECTIONS:

1. Preheat oven to 350 degrees.
2. In a large bowl, add in flour, brown sugar, and white sugar. Whisk the dry ingredients together. Then add in the eggs (already beaten), vanilla, canola oil, pecans and honey. Mix together until the batter is smooth.
3. Pour into a 9 x 13 baking pan sprayed with nonstick baking spray. Let sit for about five minutes until you start to see bubbles on top of the batter.
4. Then place in the oven for about 35 minutes, or until golden brown. You want to see a little darker brown around the edges and you will know it's done. Let cool, cut into squares and serve!

"Surprise…there is no cornmeal, but it's still called Cornbread Coffee Cake because of the texture. Steve loved to eat the corner pieces with the crispy edges." - Miss Sheila

SHOTGUN RED'S DEEP FRIED SODA BALLS

INGREDIENTS:

- 1½ Cups of Soda (we used Coke, or your choice)
- 2 Eggs (beaten)
- ¼ Cup Sugar
- ½ Tsp. Salt
- 2 Tsp. Baking Powder
- 3 Cups All-Purpose Flour
- Canola Oil
- 4 Tsp. Powdered Sugar
- 1 Tsp. Cinnamon
- 1 Can Whipped Cream
- 1 Jar Maraschino Cherries

Prep. time:
10 min

Total time:
20 min

Serves: 6

DIRECTIONS:

1. In a deep pan, add about 2 inches of oil and heat the oil to 350 degrees.

2. In a bowl, add soda, eggs, and sugar. Whisk together well until sugar is dissolved. Then in a separate bowl, whisk together the salt, baking powder, and flour and slowly stir into the soda mixture. Mix until the batter is thick and smooth.

3. Using a melon scoop (or a tablespoon) carefully drop batter balls into the hot oil and fry them until they are golden brown. Then remove them with a slotted spoon to a plate lined with paper towels.

4. In a small bowl, mix together the powdered sugar and cinnamon. Then sprinkle the soda balls with the powdered sugar mixture while they are still hot. Serve in a tall glass and top with whipped cream and a maraschino cherry!

GRANNY'S BLUEBERRY PINEAPPLE COBBLER

Prep. time: 10 min | Total time: 35 min | Serves: 6

INGREDIENTS:

- 1 Stick Salted Butter (melted)
- 1 Cup Self-Rising Flour
- 1 Cup White Sugar
- 1 Cup Whole Milk
- 1 Cup Fresh or Frozen Blueberries (thawed)
- 1 15oz. Can Crushed Pineapple in 100% Pineapple Juice (You can also use tidbits or chunks)

DIRECTIONS:

1. Preheat oven to 350 degrees.
2. In a 9 x 12 glass baking dish, pour in melted butter (brush a little of the butter up the sides of the dish).
3. In a bowl, whisk together the self-rising flour, and sugar. Then slowly pour in the milk and stir until well combined.
4. Pour the batter over the melted butter in the baking dish (do not stir).
5. Then pour the pineapple and blueberries evenly over the top (again do not stir). Sprinkle some sugar over the top.

6. Bake in the oven for 30 to 35 minutes, or until the crust is golden brown.
7. Let cool for 10 to 15 minutes. Then serve with whipped cream, or your favorite vanilla ice cream!

BAMA PEANUT BRITTLE

Prep. time: 10 min | Total time: 10 min | Serves: 12

INGREDIENTS:

- ½ Cup Water
- 1 Cup Sugar
- ¼ Cup Light Corn Syrup
- 1 Cup "Raw" Peanuts
- 1 Tsp. Butter
- 1 Tsp. Vanilla
- 1 Tsp. Baking Soda
- Nonstick Cooking Spray

DIRECTIONS:

1. Spray a cookie sheet with nonstick cooking spray and set aside.
2. In a medium saucepan, add water, sugar, and corn syrup and bring it to a boil. Boil for 3 minutes, then add raw peanuts and continue to boil stirring constantly until the peanuts turn golden brown (about 5 minutes).
3. Once the peanuts get golden brown, remove from the heat, and quickly add 1 tsp. butter, 1 tsp. vanilla, and 1 tsp. baking soda. Only stir for 10 more seconds.
4. Pour the peanut brittle mixture onto the cookie sheet, but do not smooth it out. Let it flatten on its own (this will keep the air bubbles in the peanut brittle which gives it a delicate texture). You can tilt the cookie sheet slightly to help it flatten out, but do not stir or spread with a spoon. Let it cool completely to room temperature, then break it into 2 to 3 inch pieces.

MOM'S OLD FASHIONED PEACH GELATIN DESSERT

INGREDIENTS:

- 2 Small Boxes Peach Gelatin Mix
- 2 Cups Boiling Hot Water
- 1 Large Can Peach Pie Filling or Fresh Sliced Peaches
- 1 Small Can Crushed Pineapple (drained)

Topping:
- 1 8oz. Cream Cheese Box (softened)
- 1 8oz. Sour Cream
- ¾ Cups Sugar

Prep. time: 10 min | Total time: 3-4 hours | Serves: 8

DIRECTIONS:

1. In a medium-large bowl, add peach gelatin mix. Pour in hot water and stir together until gelatin is dissolved.
2. Then stir in fresh sliced peaches or peach pie filling, and crushed pineapple.
3. Put in the refrigerator for 3 hours, or until it sets up.
4. To make the topping, in a medium bowl add cream cheese, sour cream, and sugar. Blend together with an electric mixer. Then spread on top of the chilled/set peach gelatin, and sprinkle with chopped pecans.
5. Chill for another 30 minutes and serve.

PECAN STICKY BUNS WITH CREAM CHEESE

INGREDIENTS:

- 2 Sticks Butter (melted and divided)
- 1 Cup Chopped Pecans
- 1 Cup Maple Syrup
- 1 Can Big Biscuits (8 Pack)
- 1 8oz. Box Cream Cheese
- ¼ Cup Cinnamon
- ¾ Cup Sugar
- Nonstick Baking Spray

Prep. time: 10 min

Total time: 40 min

Serves: 8

DIRECTIONS:

1. Preheat oven to 350 degrees.
2. In a bundt pan sprayed with nonstick baking spray, pour in 1 stick of melted butter (pour the other stick of melted butter into a small bowl and set aside). Then add the chopped pecans evenly over the melted butter in the bundt pan, and then pour the maple syrup over the pecans.
3. Take half a block of cream cheese and cut it up into 8 equal pieces. Then set aside.
4. In a small bowl, mix together the sugar and cinnamon. Then set aside.
5. Flatten each biscuit to about ¼ inch thick. Then roll the cream cheese pieces into the cinnamon sugar mixture and place 1 piece in the center of each biscuit.
6. Shape each biscuit into a ball around the cream cheese. Then roll each biscuit in the melted butter and then into the cinnamon sugar mixture.
7. Place the biscuits evenly in the bundt pan on top of the butter, syrup, and pecans.
8. Bake for 35 to 40 minutes, or until golden brown. Let cool for a couple of minutes, then invert onto a serving plate and serve.

MOM'S HOMEMADE COCONUT PIE

INGREDIENTS:

- 1 Pie Crust (ready to bake)
- 1 ¼ Cups Sugar
- ¼ Cup Self-Rising Flour
- 4 Eggs (divided: 3 yolks, 4 whites)
- 2 Cups Milk
- ½ Stick Butter
- 2 Cups Sweetened Shredded Coconut (divided)
- 2 Tsp. Vanilla
- ¼ Tsp. Cream of Tartar

Prep. time:
15 min

Total time:
4 hours

Serves: 6

DIRECTIONS:

1. Preheat oven to 400 degrees.
2. Poke the bottom of the pie crust with a fork so that it does not bubble up. Then bake it in the oven for 8 to 10 minutes (depending on your oven) until the crust is lightly golden brown. Remove it from the oven and let it cool.
3. In two bowls, separate 3 eggs placing the yolks in one bowl, and the egg whites in another. Place the bowl with the egg whites aside. Then in the bowl with the egg yolks, add 1 cup of sugar, and ¼ cup of flour. Whisk together until well mixed.
4. Then stir in the milk a little at a time and add the butter. Microwave the bowl for 5 to 6 minutes to melt the butter, stirring every couple of minutes until it's completely melted and mixed. Remove the bowl from the microwave and stir in 1 ½ cups of coconut and 1 tsp. of vanilla. Then pour the mixture into the pie crust.

Making the Meringue:

5. In the bowl with the egg whites, add one more egg white. Whip the egg whites with an electric mixer on high speed until they form soft peaks.
6. Then turn the speed down to low and add ¼ cup of sugar, ¼ tsp. cream of tartar, and 1 tsp. of vanilla, and continue to beat until the egg whites form stiff peaks.
7. Top the pie with the meringue, and gently spoon and spread the meringue over the pie to the edge of the crust and sprinkle with coconut.
8. Place in the oven and bake at 400 degrees for 3 to 4 minutes, or until the meringue turns golden brown. Remove from the oven and let cool on a wire rack for about 1 hour.

Made in the USA
Monee, IL
12 June 2021

71101579R00067